FORAGING CALIFORNIA

FORAGING CALIFORNIA

Finding, Identifying, and Preparing
Edible Wild Foods in California

Second Edition

Christopher Nyerges

GUILFORD, CONNECTICUT
HELENA, MONTANA

FALCONGUIDES®

An imprint of The Rowman & Littlefield Publishing Group, Inc.
4501 Forbes Blvd., Ste. 200
Lanham, MD 20706
www.rowman.com
Falcon and FalconGuides are registered trademarks and Make Adventure Your Story is a
trademark of The Rowman & Littlefield Publishing Group, Inc.

Distributed by NATIONAL BOOK NETWORK

Photos by Christopher Nyerges, except where otherwise noted
Chart on page 10 by Thomas Elpel, reprinted with permission

Map by The Rowman & Littlefield Publishing Group, Inc.

British Library Cataloguing in Publication Information available

Library of Congress Cataloging-in-Publication Data available
Names: Nyerges, Christopher, author.
Title: Foraging california : finding, identifying, and preparing edible wild foods in california /
Christopher Nyerges.
Description: Second edition. | Guilford, Connecticut : FalconGuides, [2019] | Includes index.
Identifiers: LCCN 2019005481 (print) | LCCN 2019006772 (ebook) | ISBN 9781493040902
(Electronic) | ISBN 9781493040896 (paperback : alk. paper) | ISBN 9781493040902 (ebook)
Subjects: LCSH: Wild plants, Edible. | Wild plants, Edible—California. | Wild plants, Edible—
California, Northern. | Wild plants, Edible—California, Southern. | Wild plants, Edible—
California—Identification. | Wild plants, Edible—California, Northern—Identification. | Wild
plants, Edible—California, Southern—Identification. | Cooking (Wild foods)
Classification: LCC QK98.5.U6 (ebook) | LCC QK98.5.U6 N938 2019 (print) | DDC
581.6/32—dc23
LC record available at https://lccn.loc.gov/2019005481

∞™ The paper used in this publication meets the minimum requirements of American National
Standard for Information Sciences—Permanence of Paper for Printed Library Materials, ANSI/
NISO Z39.48-1992.

Printed in the United States of America

Dr. Leonid Enari, my teacher, mentor, and friend

CONTENTS

Acknowledgments xi
Introduction 1
Plants Listed by Environment Type 3
Collecting and Harvesting Wild Foods 8
How Much Wild Food Is Out There, Anyway? 10
Are Wild Foods Nutritious?. 12

MUSHROOMS 15
Basidiomycetes 18
    Chicken-of-the-Woods (*Laetiporus sulphureus*) 18
    Shaggy Mane / Inky Cap (*Coprinus comatus*) 21
    Lepiota (*Lepiota rhacodes*) 23
    Oyster Mushroom (*Pleurotus ostreatus*) 25
Ascomycetes 27
    Morels (*Morchella esculenta*) 27

SEAWEEDS 29
Marine Green Algae (Chlorophyta); Brown Algae (Phaeophyta); Red Algae
(Rhodophyta). 30

FERNS 33
Bracken Family (Dennstaedtiacea) 34
    Bracken (*Pteridium aquilinum*) 34

GYMNOSPERMS 37
Ephedra Family (Ephedraceae) 38
    Mormon Tea (*Ephedra* spp.) 38
Pine Family (Pinaceae) 41
    Pine (*Pinus* spp.) 41

MAGNOLIIDS 43
Laurel Family (Lauraceae). 44
    California Bay (*Umbellularia californica*) 44

EUDICOTS 47
Muskroot Family (Adoxaceae) 48
    Elderberry (*Sambucus* spp.) 48
Fig Marigold Family (Aizoaceae) 52
    New Zealand Spinach (*Tetragonia tetragonioides*) 52

Amaranth Family (Amaranthaceae) 55
   Amaranth (*Amaranthus* spp.) 55
Carrot Family (Apiaceae) 58
   Fennel (*Foeniculum vulgare*) 58
Sunflower Family (Asteraceae) 61
   Chicory (*Cichorium intybus*) 61
   Prickly Lettuce (*Lactuca serriola* and others) 64
   Sow Thistle (*Sonchus oleraceus* and others) 67
   Dandelion (*Taraxacum officinale*) 70
Mustard Family (Brassicaceae) 73
   Mustard (*Brassica* spp. and *Hirschfeldia incana*) 73
   Sea Rocket (*Cakile edentula* and *C. maritima*) 76
   Indian Cabbage (*Calanthus inflatus*) 79
   Shepherd's Purse (*Capsella bursa-pastoris*) 82
   Watercress (*Nasturtium officinale*) 84
   Wild Radish (*Raphanus sativus* and *R. raphanistrum*) 87
   Hedge Mustard (*Sisymbrium irio* and *S. officinale*) 90
Cactus Family (Cactaceae) 93
   Prickly Pear (*Opuntia* spp.) 93
Pink Family (Caryophyllaceae) 99
   Chickweed (*Stellaria media*) 99
Goosefoot Family (Chenopodiaceae) 103
   Orach (*Atriplex californica*) 103
   Lamb's Quarter, White and Green (*Chenopodium album* and *C. murale*) . . . 106
   Glasswort or Pickleweed (*Salicornia* spp.) 109
   Russian Thistle (*Salsola tragus*) 112
Stonecrop Family (Crassulaceae) 115
   Live-Forever (*Dudleya* spp.) 115
Heath Family (Ericaceae) 117
   Manzanita (*Arctostaphylos* spp.) 117
Legume Family (Fabaceae) 120
   Acacia (*Acacia* spp.) 120
   Carob (*Ceratonia siliqua*) 123
   Palo Verde (*Parkinsonia microphylla* and *P. florida*) 126
   Mesquite (*Prosopis glandulosa*) and Screwbean (*P. pubescens*) 129
Oak Family (Fagaceae) 132
   Oak Tree (*Quercus* spp.) 132
Geranium Family (Geraniaceae) 136
   Filaree (*Erodium* spp.) 136

Gooseberry Family (Grossulariaceae) 138
    Currants and Gooseberries (*Ribes* spp.). 138
Walnut Family (Juglandaceae) 141
    Black Walnut (*Juglans californica* and *J. hindsii*) 141
Mint Family (Lamiaceae) 144
    Mint (*Mentha* spp.) 144
    Chia (*Salvia columbariae*) 146
Mallow Family (Malvaceae). 149
    Mallow (*Malva neglecta*) 149
Miner's Lettuce Family (Montiaceae) 152
    Miner's Lettuce (*Claytonia perfoliata*) 152
Oxalis Family (Oxalidaceae) 155
    Sour Grass / Wood Sorrel (*Oxalis* spp.). 155
Passionflower Family (Passifloraceae) 158
    Passionflower (*Passiflora caerulea* and *P. tarminiana*) 158
Lopseed Family (Phrymaceae) 161
    Common Mimulus (*Mimulus guttatus*) 161
Plantain Family (Plantaginaceae) 163
    Veronica (aka Speedwell) (*Veronica americana*) 163
Buckwheat Family (Polygonaceae) 165
    California Buckwheat (*Eriogonum fasciculatum*) 165
    Curly Dock (*Rumex crispus*) 168
    Sheep Sorrel (*Rumex acetosella*). 172
    Wild Rhubarb (*Rumex hymenosepalus*) 174
Purslane Family (Portulacaceae). 176
    Purslane (*Portulaca oleracea*) and Desert Portulaca (*P. halimoides*) 176
Buckthorn Family (Rhamnaceae) 179
    California Coffee Berry (*Frangula californica* and *F. purshiana*). 179
Rose Family (Rosaceae) 181
    Toyon (*Heteromeles arbutifolia*). 181
    Wild Cherries (*Prunus* spp.) 183
    Wild Rose (*Rosa* spp.) 186
    Blackberry (*Rubus* spp.) 189
Jojoba Family (Simmondsiaceae) 191
    Jojoba (*Simmondsia chinensis*) 191
Nightshade Family (Solanaceae) 193
    Western Nightshade, Black Nightshade (*Solanum americanum*
    [aka *S. nodiflorum*], *S. douglasii*, *S. nigrum*, and *S. xanti*). 193
Nasturtium Family (Tropaeolaceae). 196

Nasturtium (*Tropaeolum majus*) 196
Nettle Family (Urticaceae) 199
    Stinging Nettle (*Urtica dioica*) 199
Grape Family (Vitaceae) 203
    Wild Grape (*Vitis* spp.) 203

MONOCOTS 206
Century Plant Family (Agavaceae) 207
    Yucca (*Hesperoyucca whipplei*) 207
Onion or Garlic Family (Alliaceae) 211
    Wild Onions et al. (*Allium* spp.) 211
Palm Family (Arecaceae) 215
    California Fan Palm (*Washingtonia filifera*) 216
Spiderwort Family (Commelinaceae) 219
    Wandering Jew (*Tradescantia fluminensis*) 219
    Tropical Spiderwort (*Commelina benghalensis*) 221
Rush Family (Juncaceae) 223
    Rush (*Juncus textilis* et al.) 223
Grass Family (Poaceae) 225
Cattail Family (Typhaceae) 228
    Cattail (*Typha* spp.) 228

Other Edibles 232
Getting Started 234
Test Your Knowledge of Plants 237
The Dozen Easiest-to-Recognize, Most Widespread, Most Versatile Wild Foods
    of California 241
Staff of Life: Best Wild-Food Bread Sources 244
Sweet Tooth: Best Wild-Food Sugars and Desserts 248
Useful References 251
Index 254
Recipe Index 259
About the Author 260

ACKNOWLEDGMENTS

After I had already spent several years learning botany and ethnobotany in high school and college, books and lectures, often very piecemeal and second-hand, I had the very good fortune in 1974, approximately, to meet Dr. Leonid Enari, the senior biologist at the Los Angeles County Arboretum, who was teaching his course on "Edible, Medicinal, and Poisonous Plants." His knowledge was astronomical, and after I took several of his courses, he always allowed me to come to his office, where he would identify the various plants I brought him and tell me their stories. Never once did I bring him a plant that he didn't know. In most cases, he knew *several* stories about each plant. He eagerly worked with me on my first book, and he assisted me in compiling lists of safe and primarily edible plant families. His unique background in botany and chemistry made him ideally suited as a primary source of information. He acted as my teacher, mentor, and friend, and he always encouraged my studying and teaching in this field. I felt a great loss when he passed away in 2006 at age eighty-nine. Thus, it is to Dr. Enari that I dedicate this book, *Foraging California*.

At the same time I met Dr. Enari, I met Mr. Richard E. White, founder of the nonprofit organization WTI, and whose organization sponsored the walks that I began leading in 1974. White was instrumental in showing me how to plan activities, how to teach, and how to think.

I also had many other mentors, teachers, and supporters along the way. These include (but are not limited to) Dr. Luis Wheeler (University of Southern California botanist), Richard Barmakian (nutritionist), Dorothy Poole (Gabrielino "chaparral granny"), John Watkins (a Mensan who "knew everything"), Mr. Muir (my botany teacher at John Muir High School), Robert Tally (Los Angeles Mycological Association), William Breen (also of the Los Angeles Mycological Association, who taught me to cook with mushrooms), and Pascal Baudar and Mia Wasilevich, both wild-food cooking experts. These individuals all imparted valuable information to me, and they have all been my mentors to varying degrees; I also thank them for their influence. Euell

Christopher with Euell Gibbons in 1975

Gibbons also had a strong impact on my early studies of wild food, mostly through his books; I met him only once.

Of course, there have been many others who taught me bits and pieces along the way, and I feel gratitude for everyone whose love of the multifaceted art of ethnobotany has touched me in some way. Some of these friends and strong supporters have included Peter Gail, Gary Gonzales, Dude McLean, Alan Halcon, Paul Campbell, Rick and Karen Adams, Barbara Kolander, Jim Robertson, and Timothy Snider. I also want to extend a special thanks to my beloved wife, Helen, for her support of this project with both photos and ideas.

Photographer Rick Adams

Yes, I took many of the photos in this book, but I couldn't do it all myself. Rick Adams deserves special thanks for the many trips we took together to get photos for this book. Other folks who contributed photos include Helen Wong, Otto Gasser, Gary Gonzales, Barbara Kolander, Louis-M. Landry, Vickie Shufer, Jeff Martin, and Lily Jane Tsong.

INTRODUCTION

We owe a debt of gratitude to the generations of indigenous native Californians whose lives and livelihoods depended on plants for food and everything else. Much of this knowledge has been passed down from generation to generation, and much of it has been rediscovered by researchers.

Many of the living old ways have been lost, but the knowledge of how to utilize the plants of the land has not been entirely forgotten. Various generations have realized the great value of knowing how to identify and use what nature has provided, even though this information waxes and wanes in importance in the general viewpoint.

When there is war or depression or famine, we desire to rekindle this link to our past and hope for our future. When times are good and money flows, we forget our roots. Just fifty years ago, you were considered poor, and to be pitied, if you actually used wild foods.

With Euell Gibbons's popular foraging books in the early 1970s, the tide began to turn again, and today, everyone wants to know at least a little about our national heritage of wild foods. Everyone wants to be self-sufficient and part of the solution. Moreover, today we have an abundance of books, videos, and classes to teach us about these skills.

It is my hope to keep alive this basic tradition and to keep it alive in an ethical and sustainable way. Either by sheer popularity or in the aftermath of a serious emergency, local edible flora could be seriously wiped out if not collected with care and concern. This could be especially true in and around urban areas.

Today, in addition to the native flora, we have an abundance of introduced plants and common edible weeds, which were used for generations throughout Europe and Asia. Sometimes these introduced flora are a blessing, sometimes they are not. Because the non-native florae are so abundant, and generally regarded as unwanted "weeds," they should be considered the first choice of plants to include in your meals. The non-natives are generally not as sensitive as the natives, and they would actually survive well if carefully pruned to provide for your meals.

Scope of This Guide

Foraging California covers plants that can be used for food and that are common in California. We are not attempting to cover every single edible plant that could possibly be used for food or those that are very marginal as food. Our focus is on those wild foods that are widespread, easily recognizable and identifiable, and sufficient to create meals. Many of the wild edibles that are too localized, or only provide a marginal source of food, are not included.

This is also not a book about medicinal properties, and though some medicinal aspects will be addressed in passing, we will provide some ideal references in the rear of the book for such exploration. Nor is this book focusing exclusively on native plants. If you're hungry in the woods, or your own backyard, you don't care if the plant is native or introduced, right?

Organization of Guide

The plants in this book are organized according to the system used by botanists; we will be following *The Jepson Manual: Vascular Plants of California* (2012).

Many books on plants organize them by flower color or environmental niche, both of which have their adherents and their pitfalls. However, this book is categorizing the plants according to their families, which gives you a broader perspective on many more plants than can be reasonably put into one book. As you will see, many of the genera (and some families) are entirely safe to use as food. This is how I was taught by my teacher and mentor, Dr. Leonid Enari, because he believed that—though there is no shortcut to learning about the identity and uses of plants—understanding the families will impart a far greater insight into the scope of "wild foods."

We'll start with the "lower" plants and then the gymnosperms (the cone-bearing plants) before finishing with the flowering plants, all in alphabetical order by their Latin family names.

The concept of a "plant family" is based upon similarity of the macroscopic and microscopic features, usually the floral characteristics. Botanists observe these common characteristics in nature and call it a family. But as the years roll by, precise definitions of what makes up a particular family are refined, and botanists move plants from family to family for clarity. Within the family, the plant's name is composed of the genus name (the groups within a family) and its individual name, the species name. Unfortunately for the average plant student, botanists continually refine the genus to which a plant belongs. Therefore, if you have older books, they will reflect the understanding during that time of how the plants are related and into which group they belong. In this book, we have used the most recent Latin names of the plants, and we list older (now obsolete) names in most cases.

If you already know the plant's Latin or common name, you can look it up in the index.

Major Environment Types

In our selection of plants for *Foraging California,* we've attempted to include common edible plants from the different environments of the state. Below, you will see the broad categories of desert, chaparral, mountain, riparian, ocean, and urban. However, keep in mind that there is often a lot of overlap from one ecosystem to another. Oaks, for example, can be found everywhere. However, seaweed and glasswort will *only* be found in an ocean environment.

As a handy reference to the plants in this book, note the biological zone where each plant is most likely to be encountered. Some plants are only found in one zone, but others can be found in several of these zones.

PLANTS LISTED BY ENVIRONMENT TYPE

The state of California is a complex place. Biology texts will show the state with lines delineating one biotic zone from another, and sometimes you can find clean and distinct biotic zones. Studying these zones helps us get an idea of the biological diversity of the state. However, urban sprawl, farming, fires, grazing, and other factors have all continued to blur the clean distinctions from one zone to the other. Transition is everywhere, and plants often choose to live outside the zone where we expect them to be. Thus, the categories listed below are broad biological zones that you will find in California, with lots of overlap. These categories help you to understand the state, but their borders are not hard and fast.

Desert—The largest desert in California is the Mojave Desert, which occupies a large portion of the southeastern part of the state. East of the Sierra Nevada, there's the Great Basin, and farther south there's the Sonoran Desert. A desert is a region of limited precipitation and great temperature extremes. Plants here have adapted to little water and constant winds. Plants typical of the desert regions include creosote bush, palo verde, mesquite, the native fan palm, and a vast variety of cacti.

Cacti, 93
Chia, 146
Jojoba, 191
Indian cabbage, 79
Mesquite, 129
Mormon tea, 38
Onions, 211
Palms, 215
Palo verde, 126
Wild rhubarb, 174

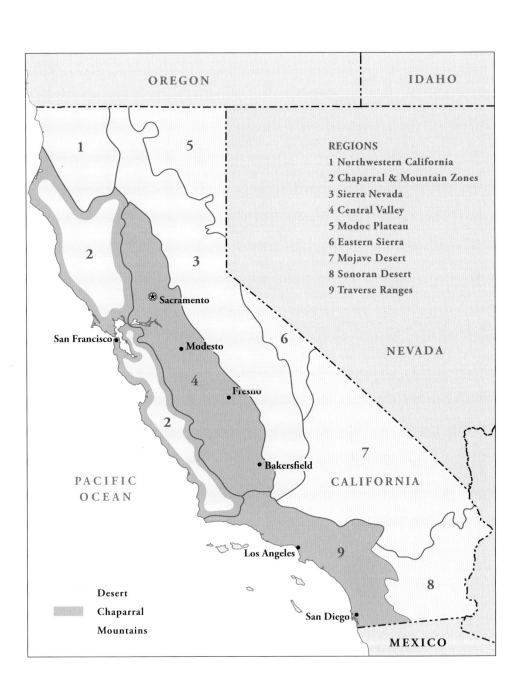

OREGON

IDAHO

1

5

REGIONS
1 Northwestern California
2 Chaparral & Mountain Zones
3 Sierra Nevada
4 Central Valley
5 Modoc Plateau
6 Eastern Sierra
7 Mojave Desert
8 Sonoran Desert
9 Traverse Ranges

2

3

⊛ Sacramento

San Francisco •

• Modesto

6

NEVADA

4

• Fresno

2

• Bakersfield

PACIFIC
OCEAN

7

CALIFORNIA

Los Angeles •

9

• San Diego

8

Desert
Chaparral
Mountains

MEXICO

(Ocean, riparian, and urban zones are pretty obvious so are not shown on this map.)

1. Northwestern California, which includes the Klamath Range and Cascade Range. This area will generally correspond to this book's Mountain Zone.
2. This includes the coastal ranges and both the Chaparral and Mountain Zones in this book, with the chaparral ranges occurring on the outer edges.
3. This is the Sierra Nevada, generally corresponding with the Mountain Zone in this book.
4. This is the Central Valley, the heart of farming. This will correspond to the Urban Zone and Chaparral Zone (on the fringes of the Central Valley) of this book.
5. The Modoc Plateau. This will generally correspond to the Desert Zone of this book.
6. This section is in the Eastern Sierra, with Great Basin influence, and generally will correspond to the Desert Zone of this book.
7. The Mojave Desert. This corresponds to the Desert Zone of this book.
8. The Sonoran Desert. This corresponds to the Desert Zone of this book.
9. This includes the Traverse Ranges of the San Gabriel and San Bernardino Mountains. This also includes the San Jacinto Mountains. These areas will roughly correspond with the Chaparral and Mountain Zones in this book.

Chaparral—Chaparral is a shrubland plant community that can be found anywhere from the ocean up to an elevation of about 5,000 feet. It has a Mediterranean climate (mild, wet winters and hot, dry summers) and wildfire. Sometimes called the Upper Sonoran Zone, this is the plant community between the desert and the mountainous regions, consisting of such plants as laurel sumac, buckwheat, yucca, white sage, and other woody shrubs. Most of the plants we've listed here are natives, but many others will be found in the chaparral, especially where developments have invaded the native terrain.

Blackberries, 189
California bay, 44
California buckwheat, 165
Wild cherry, 183
California coffee berry, 179
Elderberry, 48
Manzanita, 117
Nightshade, 193
Oak, 132
Passionflower, 158
Toyon, 181
Walnut, 141
Yucca, 207

Ocean—The ocean zone is self-evident—these are all the plants that are unique to the ocean and beach areas from Oregon south to Mexico. The ones we've listed here are somewhat exclusive to beaches when found in the wild. However, keep in mind that the interface between the ocean and the urban, chaparral, or mountain zones can be a very short distance. This means you can expect to find many other plants on and near the beaches.

Glasswort, 109
New Zealand spinach, 52
Orach, 103
Sea rocket, 76
Seaweeds, 29

Mountain—The mountainous zones are those at higher elevations with typically colder temperatures and higher winds. The plants we've included in this category are mountainous plants, but they may also be found in other zones.

Bracken, 34
Currants and gooseberries, 138
Dudleya, 115
Miner's lettuce, 152
Oak, 132
Pine, 41

Riparian—The riparian zone refers to the areas along rivers or streams and around lakes. The plants in this zone require good amounts of water, so you won't generally find them far from a water source. Most that we've included here are natives. Although the riparian regions are estimated to be about 1 to 2 percent of the total landscape, all fauna relate to and largely depend upon that very small percentage of land.

Cattails, 228
Mint, 144
Monkey flower, 161
Veronica, 163
Watercress, 84
Wild grape, 203

Urban & Field—Often considered "weeds," these are the plants of the urban environment, the valleys and fields, and the edges of farms (such as throughout the Central Valley). Nearly all of them have come here from somewhere else, and they are nature's "survivors." They grow in lawns, backyards, cracks in the sidewalks, throughout all urban areas, and on the vast fringes of the urban sprawl.

Acacia, 120
Amaranth, 55
Carob, 123
Chicory, 61
Chickweed, 99
Curly dock, 168
Dandelion, 70
Fennel, 58
Filaree, 136
Hedge mustard, 90
Lamb's quarter, 106
Mallow, 149
Mustard, 73
Nasturtium, 196
Nettle, 199
Purslane, 176
Radish, 87
Rose, 186
Russian thistle, 112
Sheep sorrel, 172
Shepherd's purse, 82
Sour grass, 155
Sow thistle, 67
Miner's lettuce, 152
Wandering Jew, 219

COLLECTING AND HARVESTING WILD FOODS

Because more and more people want to learn how to "live off the land" and use wild plants for food and medicine, please practice sustainable collecting and harvesting methods. Don't neglect the wild foods in your own yards. Moreover, if you have the space, you should grow (or allow to grow) many of the wild plants that you enjoy eating.

Always make sure it is both legal and safe for you to harvest wild foods. Legality can usually be determined simply by asking a few questions or making a phone call. Don't be surprised if you are then asked *what* you intend to pick. Because many of the plants listed in this book are often regarded as "nuisance weeds," most property owners will allow you to come in and remove the plants that they do not want.

In some cases, when we're dealing with public lands, the issue of legality might be a bit more difficult to ascertain.

You also want to be safe, making sure there are no agricultural or commercial toxins near and around the plants you intend to harvest. Again, it pays, in the long run, to carefully observe the surrounding area and to ask a few questions.

Unless it is the root that you are using for food, you should never need to uproot a plant, especially if it is only the leaves that you intend to eat. I have documented in my book *Extreme Simplicity* how I was able to extend the life of many annual weeds by carefully pinching back the leaves that I wanted to eat and then allowing the plant to grow back before picking it again. Even when I believe that someone else will pull up the plant later, or plow the area, I still do not uproot the plants on general principle. The root system is good for the soil, and if the plant's roots are left alone, it will continue to manufacture oxygen. Various insects and birds might eat the bugs on the plant or its seeds. Let life continue.

When you are harvesting greens, snippers can be used, but usually, nothing is needed but your fingernails—maybe a sharp knife. Cut what you need, don't deplete an area, and move on.

Harvesting seeds is done when the plant is at the end of its annual cycle, but that is still no reason to uproot the plant. When I harvest curly dock or lamb's quarter seed, I carefully try to get as much into my bag as possible. I know that some seed is being scattered, and that's a good thing for next season. I also know that a few seeds are still on the stalk, and that's a good thing for the birds in the area. I nearly always harvest in an area of abundance. If there are very few specimens there, my usual course of action is to simply leave them alone.

You will note when you read this text that I advise foragers to leave the wild onions in the ground and to eat the greens. In cases of abundance, your thinning of the roots will help to stimulate more growth, and that is a good thing, which is akin to the passive agricultural practices of the Native Americans who exclusively once lived here.

In sum, you must observe the legality of wherever you choose to collect wild plants. However, beyond "legality," it is my hope that you work to develop a mind-set of ethicality and sustainability as a forager. In the old times, the indigenous people automatically practiced sustainable harvesting because the alternative for not doing so was starvation! We seem to think (foolishly) that we can do whatever we wish because we have so many human-created backups. Always practice sustainable foraging. Never uproot plants if you're only eating the leaves! Don't overharvest. Only take what you need.

Foraging doesn't require many tools. You will need bags—plastic, cloth, paper—whatever is appropriate for the food item. In some cases, you will harvest with buckets or tubs. Usually, no other tools are needed, though I generally carry a Florian ratchet clipper for any cutting as well as a knife or two. I rarely need a trowel, though it comes in handy with some harvesting.

The more you forage, the more you'll realize that your best tool is your memory. You'll learn to recognize where the edible flowers grow, where the berry vines are, and the fields that will be full of chickweed next spring. And the more you know, the less you'll need to carry.

HOW MUCH WILD FOOD IS OUT THERE, ANYWAY?

Plants Everywhere, but Not All Can Be Eaten

In his book *Participating in Nature: Wilderness Survival and Primitive Living Skills,* Thomas Elpel created a unique chart, based on years of observation and analysis, to give a perspective on the sheer number of edible, medicinal, and poisonous plants. The chart is reprinted with permission in this book. Elpel is also the author of *Botany in a Day.* Simply put, this is the way botany should be taught in the colleges. Elpel brings it alive in a way that is immediately applicable.

Almost every plant with known ethnobotanical uses can be used medicinally; even some otherwise toxic plants can be used medicinally if you know the right doses and proper application. Yes, medicine is everywhere. However, a large majority of these plants are neither poisonous nor used for food for various reasons.

The extremely poisonous plants that will outright kill you are rare. Moreover, because there are so few of these deadly plants, it is not all that difficult to learn to identify them. In Southern California, for example, there is poison hemlock and castor bean, which are readily recognizable. Others that could cause death are various mushrooms, oleander, and tree tobacco, though we rarely hear about that happening.

Though there are only a few that are deadly poisonous, there are many more—perhaps five times as many plants as the very deadly ones—that would make you very sick but that would not normally kill you.

Edible, Medicinal, and Poisonous Plants

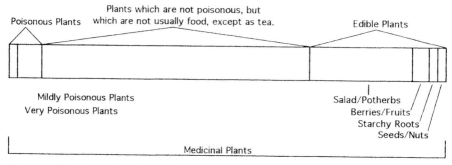

Reprinted with permission of Tom Elpel

Still, all the poisonous and toxic plants combined are a small minority of all the known ethnobotanicals.

Edible plants make up approximately one-fifth of the known edible, medicinal, and poisonous plants.

Of the plants that we normally think of as "food plants," the overwhelming majority—maybe 70 percent or so—primarily provide us with greens. That is, throughout most of the year, most of the food that you'll obtain in the wild consists of greens: food to make salads and stir-fries, and to add to soups and vegetable dishes. These are plants that by themselves will not create a filling and balanced meal, but they will add vitamins and minerals to your dried beans, MREs (meals ready to eat), freeze-dried camping food, and other foods. In general, greens are not high sources of protein, fats, or carbohydrates.

Berries and fruits make up another category of wild foods. Maybe 10 to 15 percent of the wild foods you find will provide you with berries or fruits, but timing is everything. Unlike greens, which you can usually find year-round, fruits and berries are typically available only seasonally. If you want some during other parts of the year, you'll need to dry them or make jams or preserves. This includes blackberries, elderberries, toyon, mulberries, and many others. They provide sugar and flavor, but like greens, you would not make a meal entirely from fruits and berries.

An even smaller category of wild foods, perhaps 5 to 7 percent, consists of starchy roots, such as cattails. These are great for energy, though they may not be available year-round. This is why these foods have traditionally been dried, and even powdered, and stored for later use.

Another small category of wild foods consists of seeds and nuts. Included are grass seeds, pine nuts, mesquite, screwbean, carob, acorns, and many others. It is in this small category, maybe 5 percent of wild foods, where you obtain the carbohydrates, oils, and, sometimes, proteins that constitute the "staff of life." Though these are not available all year, some have a longer harvest time than others. Others may have a harvest period of as short as two weeks. Many grass seeds simply fall to the ground and are eaten by animals. Fortunately, most of these can be harvested in season and stored for later use.

(By the way, we're using specific percentages here very guardedly. They are what we might call educated guesses. There are so many plants in the world that we know it can be troublesome when you assign specific numbers to these percentages.)

ARE WILD FOODS NUTRITIOUS?

It is a common misconception that "wild foods" are neither nutritious nor tasty. Both these points are erroneous, as anyone who has actually taken the time to identify and use wild foods can testify. I've also had many new students who had been convinced about the nutritional value of wild foods but assumed that the plants nevertheless tasted bad. Of course, a bad cook can make even the best foods unpalatable. Moreover, if you pick wild foods and don't clean them, don't use just the tender sections, and don't prepare them carefully, you certainly can turn someone off to wild foods.

My friends Pascal Baudar and Mia Wasilevich continue to use wild foods in their gourmet dishes and classes, and they have proven that wild foods are not only nutritious but can be as flavorful as any foods in the finest restaurants.

For your edification, here is a chart extracted from *Composition of Foods*, provided by the US Department of Agriculture (USDA), to give you an idea of the nutritional content of common wild foods.

Nutritional Composition of Wild Foods

The data below are per 100 grams unless otherwise indicated. Blanks denote no data available; dashes denote lack of data for a constituent believed to be present in measurable amounts. Only a select number of plants for which we had data are represented.

Plant	Calories	Protein (g)	Fat (g)	Calcium (mg)	Phosphorus (mg)	Iron (mg)	Sodium (mg)	Potassium (mg)	Vitamin A (IU)	Thiamine (mg)	Riboflavin (mg)	Niacin (mg)	Vit. C (mg)	Part
Amaranth	36	3.5	0.5	267	67	3.9	—	411	6,100	0.08	0.16	1.4	80	Leaf, raw
Carob		4.5		352	81	2.9	35	827	14		0.4	1.89	0.2	Pods
Cattail		8%	2%											Rhizomes
Chia		20.2%		631	860	7.72	16	407	54	0.62	0.17	8.8	1.6	Seed
CHICORY TRIBE														
Chicory	20	1.8	0.3	86	40	0.9	—	420	4,000	0.06	0.1	0.5	22	Leaf, raw
Dandelion	45	2.7	0.7	187	66	3.1	76	397	14,000	0.19	0.26	—	35	Leaf, raw
Sow thistle	20	2.4	0.3	93	35	3.1	—	—	2,185	0.7	0.12	0.4	5	Leaf, raw
Chickweed														
Dock	28	2.1	0.3	66	41	1.6	5	338	12,900	0.09	0.22	0.5	119	Leaf, raw
Fennel	28	2.8	0.4	100	51	2.7	—	397	3,500	—	—	—	31	Leaf, raw
Filaree	—	2.5	—	—	—	—	—	—	7,000	—	—	—	—	Leaf
Grass										300–500 IU	2,000 to 2,800 IU		300 to 700 mg	Leaf, raw
Lamb's quarter	43	4.2	0.8	309	72	1.2	43	452	11,600	0.16	0.44	1.2	80	Leaf, raw
Mallow	37	4.4	0.6	249	69	12.7	—	—	2,190	0.13	0.2	1.0	35	Leaf
Milkweed	—	0.8	0.5	—	—	—	—	—	—	—	—	—	—	Leaf
Miner's lettuce						10% RDA			22% RDA				33% RDA	Leaf
MUSTARD FAMILY														
Mustard	31	3	0.5	183	50	3	32	377	7,000	0.12	0.22	0.8	97	Leaf
Shepherd's purse	33	4.2	0.5	208	86	4.8	—	394	1,554	0.08	0.17	0.4	36	Leaf
Watercress	19	2.2	0.3	120	60	0.2	41	330	3,191		0.12	0.2	43	Leaf
Nasturtium														
Nettle	65	5.5	0.7	481	71	1.64	4	334	4,300	—	0.16	0.38	76	Leaf
New Zealand spinach	19	2.2	0.3	58	46	2.6	159	795	4,300	0.04	0.17	0.6	30	Leaf, raw
Oak (acorn flour)	65% carbohydrates	6%	18%	43	103	1.21	0	712	51	0.1	0.1	2.3	0	Nut

Plant	Calories	Protein (g)	Fat (g)	Calcium (mg)	Phosphorus (mg)	Iron (mg)	Sodium (mg)	Potassium (mg)	Vitamin A (IU)	Thiamine (mg)	Riboflavin (mg)	Niacin (mg)	Vit. C (mg)	Part
ONION FAMILY														
Chives	28	1.8	0.3	69	44	1.7	—	250	5,800	0.08	0.13	0.5	56	Leaf, raw
Garlic	137	6.2	0.2	29	202	1.5	19	529	—	0.25	0.08	0.5	15	Clove, raw
Onion	36	1.5	0.2	51	39	1	5	231	2,000	0.05	0.05	0.4	32	Young leaf, raw
Passion fruit [per pound]				31	151	3.8	66	831	1,650				71	Fruit
Pinyon	635	12	60.5		604	5.2				1.28				Nut
Prickly pear	42	0.5	0.1	20	28	0.3	2	166	60	0.01	0.03	0.4	22	Fruit, raw
Prickly Pear	16	1.2	trace	163	17	0.7	22	319	415	0.01	0.04	0.5	13	Pad
Purslane	21	30	1.7	0.4	103	39	3.5	—	—	2,500	0.03	0.1	0.5	Leaf & stem, raw
Rose	162	1.6		169	61	1.06	4	429	4,345		0.16	1.3	426	Fruit, raw
SEAWEED														
Dulse	—	—	3.2	296	267	—	2,085	8,060	—	—	—	—	—	Leaf
Irish moss	—	—	1.8	885	157	8.9	2,892	2,844	—	—	—	—	—	Leaf
Kelp	—	—	1.1	1,093	240	—	3,007	5,273	—	—	—	—	—	Leaf

Mushrooms

Fungi do not contain chlorophyll like green plants, and this means they do not manufacture their own food. They feed themselves by digesting other organic matter. They reproduce by microscopic spores, analogous to seeds of green plants. However, spores are much simpler in structure than a seed and usually consist of only one cell.

When we say "mushroom," we are referring to the fruiting body of the fungi, usually (but not always) the typical form of a stem with a cap. In favorable environments, the spores develop into many threadlike cells, called hyphae, which (again, under ideal conditions) can develop into the underground network of cobwebby material called mycelium (or spawn). This usually unseen network is the vegetative portion of the fungi, and the spore-bearing "fruits" that are produced from the mycelium are what we call mushrooms.

However, since some fungi are growths, such as bread molds, yeast molds, mildews, and even athlete's foot fungus, which never produce the fruiting growths, some fungi would never be called "mushrooms." In other words, all mushrooms are fungi, but not all fungi are mushrooms.

We're only interested in the macroscopic fungi, mushrooms, even though some of the macroscopic fungi look nothing like the conventional cap and stem mushroom.

Just like flowering plants are divided into two major divisions (the Angiosperms and the Gymnosperms), all macroscopic fungi are either Basidiomycetes or Ascomycetes, terms that describe how the spores are formed. In the Basidiomycetes, by far the larger group, the spores are formed on the outside of club-shaped cells called "basidia." With Ascomycetes, on the other hand, the spores are formed inside a sac-like "mother cell" called "asci." At this stage, you probably don't need to know the difference between Basidiomycetes and Ascomycetes, but if you proceed with the study of mycology, these are terms that you should be familiar with.

We have included only a few mushrooms that are somewhat common and easy to recognize. In fact, because this is just a "teaser" about edible mushrooms, the mushrooms included are some of the few that I typically eat when I am able to find them.

In this text, we are describing only a few individual mushrooms and are not describing the families that each of these species belongs to or their relations to each other. To get that fuller (and necessary) picture, we strongly advise that you enroll in a course in mycology, or get David Arora's *Mushrooms Demystified,* which gives you an excellent overview of the science of mycology.

We won't take time here to describe all the parts of a "typical" mushroom because the ones we've chosen here are not all "typical." For those desiring that sort of technical information, we suggest the aforementioned *Mushrooms Demystified.*

A good beginning is the "Foolproof Four," a term coined by Clyde Christensen in his book *Common Edible Mushrooms* (University of Minnesota Press, 1947). The Foolproof Four are chicken-of-the-woods, morels, puffballs, and the shaggy mane (an inky cap). Beginning mycology students would do well to master these four and their families. These (and other common fungi) are widely described in mycological literature.

Richard Redman examines a chicken-of-the-woods mushroom growing from a eucalyptus stump in his yard.

CHICKEN-OF-THE-WOODS
Laetiporus sulphureus (aka *Polyporus sulphureus* and *Grifola sulphureus*)

Use: Edible and good when properly prepared
Range: Widespread
Similarity to toxic species: None
Best time: Fall
Status: Common, in season
Tools needed: Knife, collecting bag

A close-up view of the chicken-of-the-woods mushroom LILY JANE TSONG

Properties

This is an easy-to-recognize shelf fungus that is fairly widespread in the fall. It grows in layers, or horizontal "shelves," on various host trees, typically carob and eucalyptus, but it can also be found on oak, plum, hemlock, and spruce in California. It will grow on living trees and downed stumps. When young, the lower layer appears to be a solid yellow surface, but it is actually covered with minute pores (no gills, as with other mushrooms),

A top view of chicken-of-the-woods growing on a carob tree LILY JANE TSONG

and it is usually bright yellow. The top of the shelves will be colored in layers from the outside in, from yellow, to orange, to nearly red. As it ages, the shelves become nearly white; at that stage, they have become inedible.

Students Sarah Shin, Madison Franco, and Morgan Clark (from the left) examine a chicken-of-the-woods they just found at the base of a eucalyptus tree.

Uses

Cut off only the most tender outer sections of this mushroom. Though some people have merely sautéed the fresh tender portions of this mushroom with no ill effects, most of us need to do a more thorough preparation. I prepared them as I was taught by one of my mushroom mentors, William Breen. First, we'd cut the chicken-of-the-woods into bite-size pieces, approximately one- to two-inch squares. We'd then boil it all and pour off the first water. We'd give it fresh water, boil again, and change the water. Usually, we would do a third boiling but not always. Then, one method of preparation is to simply sauté in butter and enjoy. However, following Breen's guidance, we typically coated the boiled mushroom pieces in flour, dipped them in beaten eggs, and then rolled them into crushed bread or crackers before deep-frying. Yes, you're right—deep-frying isn't the best thing for your health, but these were really awesome! These days, I usually triple boil and sauté gently with a little butter and flour in a skillet. Sometimes we sauté with sliced onions or wild greens.

If you're going to preserve these, do at least one boil and then freeze. These do not reconstitute well if you dry them.

An inky cap, also called "lawyers wig," *Coprinus comatus* MICHAEL BEDDARD

SHAGGY MANE / INKY CAP
Coprinus comatus

Use: Edible cooked when young
Range: Widespread when conditions are right; often found on wood stumps or in wood chips
Similarity to toxic species: None
Best time: When young; fall through spring
Status: Common
Tools needed: Knife, basket

Properties

Shaggy mane is but one of the "inky caps," all of which are easily recognized by the caps that "melt" into a drippy, black mass of spores. The shaggy mane is the largest of the inky caps, growing perhaps 5"–6" tall. The white cap is flaked with brown scales and is very cylindrically shaped. As it matures, the cap eventually becomes strands of black spores, dripping from the top of an erect white stem.

Uses

These must be collected while still young. To determine age, cut the mushroom in half longitudinally. You will see the hollow stem and the condition of the cap. As the cap matures, it turns from white, to pink, to black. You only want to eat the white portions; therefore, cut off and discard the rest.

As the inky cap matures, the cap appears as "melting" ink from the still-erect stem.

Though these are highly prized, they have a distinctive flavor that some people enjoy and others do not. There are many ways to prepare these. My common method is to sauté gently in butter and serve on toast.

Cautions

People have experienced gastrointestinal distress (such as vomiting) when consuming *Coprinus atramentarius* with alcohol. Though this effect has primarily been noted with *C. atramentarius,* regular consumers of alcohol tend to avoid all *Coprinus* species.

Two *Lepiota rhacodes* in the field. Note how the brown coloration on the cap breaks into flakes of brown as the cap grows.

LEPIOTA
Lepiota rhacodes (aka *Macrolepiota rhacodes* and *Chlorophyllum rhacodes*)

Use: Edible, cooked in various ways

Range: Typically grows under oak trees

Similarity to toxic species: Superficially; a poisonous *Amanita* could be confused with this one. However, another *Lepiota* can be confused with this edible one. Green gill (*Lepiota molybdites*, aka *Chlorophyllum molybdites*) is a close relative, but it tends to grow in lawns and fields. Cap is similar but a bit less substantial. Distinct umbo on cap. Gills mature to a faded green color. Some people eat this one, but it tends to cause gastrointestinal distress for most people, so it's best avoided.

Best time: Fall through spring

Status: Relatively common

Tools needed: Knife, collecting box

A young, newly emerging *Lepiota rhacodes*.
Note the bulbous base and the gill covering that
becomes the ring on the stem.

A mature *Lepiota rhacodes*. Note the bulbous
base.

Properties

It has a bulbous stem but no cup. The young mushroom has a stout stem and
a veil that covers the gills, which become a ring on the stem as the mushroom
grows. The young cap is brown, and as the cap grows, the layer of brown breaks
into scattered fragments of brown on a mostly white cap. When you slice the
mushroom in half, you will see a hollow stem and white flesh, which quickly
oxidizes to a red or rust color. The gills are white, as are the spores.

Uses

Tasty once simply sautéed. We've also sautéed it and added to cooked onions and
other greens. For a simple dish that doesn't mask the subtle flavor, gently sauté in
butter and add a little flour to the skillet; cook until browned.

A cluster of oyster mushrooms growing on a cottonwood tree

OYSTER MUSHROOM
Pleurotus ostreatus

Use: Edible cooked
Range: Widespread, growing on dead or living trees, preferring willow, cottonwood, elm, alder, and sycamore
Similarity to toxic species: Other *Pleurotus* (also *Panus* and other related fungi) can appear similar to *P. ostreatus*. Species of other genera could also bear a superficial resemblance to *P. ostreatus*. As usual, don't eat any mushroom if you aren't 100 percent certain of its identity.
Best time: Favors cool weather in the fall and winter
Status: Common
Tools needed: Knife, basket

Kevin Sutherland inspects some cultivated oyster mushrooms. Note the color of the cap compared to the wild oyster mushrooms.

Properties

Cap: Cap color varies from white, to tan, to dark brown, to nearly pink.

Spores: White. Sometimes you will see the white spores that have dropped from an oyster mushroom onto the tree, or other mushrooms, just underneath.

Gills: Decurrent, sloping down to meet the stem; white.

Stem (cup/ring): The stem is off-center and sometimes essentially absent, as this will grow directly out of the tree or stump.

Uses

These are commonly picked from the trees with the woodier base removed and the rest typically sliced and gently sautéed. They are mild-flavored and will go well with most

Young beautiful oyster mushrooms emerging from a cottonwood tree

dishes. If you collect more than what you can eat right away, you can preserve it by drying (the preferred method) or by freezing.

ASCOMYCETES

This morel grew out of ash and charcoal in Los Angeles County.

MORELS
Morchella esculenta

Use: Edible and highly prized
Range: Morels are known to prefer burned-over areas, especially burned-over conifers. They're also sometimes found in urban areas in discarded drywall.
Similarity to toxic species: There are many morels, as well as so-called "false" morels. If you're uncertain that what you've found is what's pictured here, don't eat it.
Best time: Late winter and spring
Status: Sometimes common locally
Tools needed: Knife, collecting basket

Properties
Some have described morel as a hollow sponge. That's a good analogy. There are a cap and stalk, and the cap and stalk are, essentially, a complete unit, with the cap

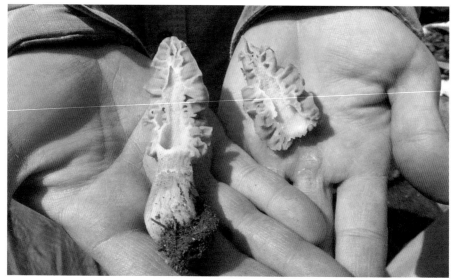
Note that the entire morel is hollow.

and stalk completely intergrown. The entire mushroom is hollow. The cap is round to oval, even cone-shaped, and honeycombed with pits and ridges, which gives rise to the sponge analogy. These pits and ridges of the cap are tan to yellowish brown, lightening up a bit as the mushroom matures. The spores are formed on the exposed surfaces of the cap.

Uses

Morels should not be eaten raw because they can cause an upset stomach and vomiting. Heat cooks off the toxic principle. Since these are hollow, they are commonly stuffed with rice or meat and baked. They can also be sautéed and served with butter or other seasonings. Often, they are added to stews.

A few morels collected from a burned-over area

William Breen prepared morels in a variety of ways, but he always emphasized that before doing anything with morels, boil them first! This was his cardinal rule to avoid sickness.

Seaweeds

Seaweed can refer to any of the macroscopic marine algae belonging to the brown algae, red algae, and green algae groups. Some tuft-forming members of the blue-green algae are also called seaweeds. The appearance of seaweeds can somewhat resemble terrestrial plants by having a stemlike structure called a stipe, a holdfast (instead of roots) that attaches to a rock or other surface, a leaf-like structure called the blade (or lamina), and a sorus (or spore cluster) instead of seeds.

Christopher Nyerges examines some kelp. RICK ADAMS

MARINE GREEN ALGAE
Chlorophyta (About 5,000 species, including sea lettuce)

BROWN ALGAE
Phaeophyta (Approximately 1,000 species, including all kelps, rockweed, etc.)

RED ALGAE
Rhodophyta (The most abundant seaweed in the world, with more than 4,000 species, including Irish moss, dulse, laver, etc.)

Use: Food (depending on species, some are eaten dried, cooked, raw, or pickled), nutrition, utility
Range: Restricted to the ocean
Similarity to toxic species: See Cautions.
Best time: Available year-round
Status: Relatively common
Tools needed: Bucket, gloves

Properties

Most people know seaweeds when they see them at the beach, floating in the surf, lying on the beach. They grow in a large array of colors, sizes, and shapes. The kelps are perhaps the most conspicuous along the California coast, with their long stipes and characteristic fronds. They often lie en masse on the beach. Moreover, the farther north one goes, the greater the diversity.

In general, the seaweeds have leaflike fronds, stipes that resemble the stems of terrestrial plants, and holdfasts that resemble roots. Some seaweeds are very delicate, and others are very tough and almost leathery. Many have hollow sections—"floats"—that allow them to float more readily.

Others are like thin sheets of wet plastic, such as the sea lettuce. Their colors generally indicate their category of green, brown, or red marine algae.

Kelp washed ashore RICK ADAMS

Uses

Seaweeds are not only tasty (when prepared properly), but they are also very nutritious.

When I was originally researching seaweeds, I spoke with botanists, marine biologists, and even a seaweed specialist. Some believed that all seaweeds—all the thousands of varieties—are a completely nontoxic group of plants, and most agreed that these are safe to consume. The more conservative viewpoint had to do with the fact that there are so many seaweeds and not all have been studied enough to make such a blanket statement. Nevertheless, seaweeds are regarded as highly nutritious and generally edible. For example, 100 g of kelp contains 1,093 mg of calcium, 240 mg of phosphorus, and 5,273 mg of potassium! And these iodine-rich foods can be used in a variety of ways. Some—such as sea lettuce, which actually looks like lettuce—can be washed and added raw to salads. Others are best dried and then used as a seasoning for other foods. Some seaweeds can be diced and added to soups and stews. Moreover, most can be simply dried and powdered and then used as a salt substitute or flavor enhancer.

If you live near the coast and have easy access to seaweeds, I encourage you to research the many specific seaweeds that are used for food and—via the many books exclusively about seaweeds—learn the many ways to prepare them.

The seaweed anchors itself to rocks via its holdfasts RICK ADAMS

And experiment! Unless you are lost and don't have the time to experiment or research, there are many sources of information today with specific recipes and methods of preparation for seaweeds.

We've made some very delicious pickles by taking the floats from kelp—the swollen, hollow bubble at the base of each frond—and soaking them in jalapeño juice or other pickling liquids. They take on the flavor of whatever they are seasoned with.

Cautions

Here are some of the common sense precautions you should take if you're going to try some seaweeds: Never eat any seaweed that has been sitting on the beach, rotting and attracting flies. Examine the seaweed; never eat seaweed that has some sort of foreign growth on it. Moreover, perhaps the hardest part of all this is that you should not consume seaweed from polluted waters; unfortunately, much of the Southern California coastline south of Malibu should be considered polluted. This means that you have to use some common sense when collecting seaweed for food, and you should thoroughly wash any seaweed that you intend to eat.

Ferns

Ferns are flowerless plants with feathery or leafy fronds. They reproduce by spores, contained in sporangia that appear as brown dots on the underside of the fronds. They are found throughout tropical to temperate regions, characterized by true roots produced from a rhizome. There are 13 families of ferns.

BRACKEN FAMILY (DENNSTAEDTIACEA)

Among the ferns, the Bracken family contains about 11 genera and about 170 species. The Bracken family's only representative in California is the bracken or brake fern.

Bracken leaf

BRACKEN
Pteridium aquilinum

Use: Young, uncurling shoots used for food
Range: Throughout the state, mostly in the shady areas of the mountains and canyons
Similarity to toxic species: See Cautions.
Best time: Spring
Status: Somewhat common in the correct terrain
Tools needed: Clippers

Properties

Bracken can apparently be found worldwide. Ours can be found throughout the state in pastures, hillsides, wooded areas, and even in full sun. You'll find it most commonly on the north, shady side of hillsides or shady hillsides where water seeps and little sun gets through the canopy of whatever larger trees grow there.

The rhizomes are hairy and sprawling underground, sometimes branching. The black petiole near the base has dense brown hairs. The plants grow 1'–4' tall, and the overall appearance of each frond is roughly triangular; each is twice-pinnately divided.

Uses

The young shoots are the edible portion, and they have the appearance of the head of a fiddle, which is where the common name "fiddlehead" comes from. The young shoots will uncurl and grow into the full fern fronds. These are picked when young and can be eaten raw or cooked. I like to toss a few fiddleheads in salads when they are in season; they impart a nutty flavor.

Bracken fiddlehead BARBARA KOLANDER

More commonly, fiddleheads are boiled or steamed and served with butter or cheese. They are easy to recognize and have gained a resurgence of popularity as more people are rediscovering wild foods. Bracken is also a good vegetable to add to soups and stews and mixed dishes. Carefully pinch off the tender, unfolding top, and you can gently rub off the hair. Use as a nibble or cook it.

Do not eat the fully opened ferns.

Cautions

Researchers have identified a substance called ptaquiloside in bracken fern, a known carcinogen. Is it safe to eat? It has been a food staple of Native Americans for centuries, if not millennia, and the Japanese also enjoy bracken and consider it one of the delicacies of spring. Although actual scientific data is inconclusive, there is a higher rate of intestinal cancer among Native Americans and the Japanese, and this could be linked to the use of bracken fern. Livestock has been known to be mildly poisoned by eating quantities of raw bracken ferns. Cooking is known to remove some of the toxins, though not necessarily the ptaquiloside.

Despite this, there are many who are not so concerned about such inconclusive studies. For example, Steven Brill, in his book *Identifying and Harvesting Edible and Medicinal Plants in Wild (and Not So Wild) Places*, states, "I wouldn't be afraid of eating reasonable quantities of wild [bracken] fiddleheads during their short season." Green Deane, another forager from Florida, says, "I am willing to risk a few fiddleheads with butter once or twice a spring, which is about as often as I can collect enough in this warm place."

A small fiddlehead RICK ADAMS

The final choice is up to you. For perspective, we regularly hear things far worse than the above about coffee, high fructose corn syrup, sugar, and french fries, yet people seem to have no problem purchasing and eating these substances. That doesn't make them good for you, but eating some in moderation is not likely to be the sole cause of cancer or other illnesses.

Gymnosperms

This is a class of plants whose naked seeds are formed in cones (as with a pine tree) or on stalks (as with *Ephedra*).

The members of this group include the cycadophytes, conifers, ginkgo, and ephedras.

EPHEDRA FAMILY (EPHEDRACEAE)

The Ephedra family consists of only one genus, *Ephedra*, with about fifty species worldwide. Seven of the *Ephedra* species are found in California; all but one are native.

Ephedra stems and little cones RICK ADAMS

MORMON TEA
Ephedra spp.

Use: Beverage
Range: The high and low deserts of Southern California
Similarity to toxic species: None, but be careful. Mormon tea looks like leafless sticks. Be attentive. While we aren't aware of a toxic look-alike, there very well could be a toxic plant that has lost its leaves and, therefore, resembles Mormon tea.
Best time: Year-round
Status: Relatively widespread
Tools needed: Clippers

Ephedra cones RICK ADAMS

Properties

Mormon tea grows in the desert, often in the driest soils where there are few other plants growing. It grows in sand drifts and sand flats, amid the creosote and the mesquite. It's a real survivor.

Moreover, when most folks look at this very unassuming plant that rises only 1'–2' out of the ground, they think they're looking at some sticks of a dead plant. However, the plant *is* all sticks! It's a gymnosperm, which makes it akin to pine trees and conifers. The plant produces tiny little cones, which actually flower, but you have to look close—and at the right time—to see them. You'll see one to five of these cones per node.

There are 7 species of *Ephedra* in California, and frankly, after you've seen one *Ephedra,* you'll recognize them all, even though there is some variety between the nuances of color, the overall size, and the way the "sticks" grow. A Mormon tea aficionado will easily see those differences, but to the average person passing through, they are all the same.

Uses

Often when camping out in California's deserts where the Mormon tea is ubiquitous, we have cut a handful of the stems and brewed them in a kettle over the fire. It's best when the kettle is covered so you don't boil away all the flavor. The resultant tea has a slightly pinkish color and a subtle flavor. It can be compared to a mild green tea, though without any strong stimulants. It makes a good evening beverage, which I prefer unsweetened so I can taste its subtle flavor. For those who prefer sweetened teas, just a half teaspoon of honey is sufficient.

Christopher examines an *Ephedra* patch. RICK ADAMS

The name of this plant came from early Mormon settlers who drank a tea made from this plant because they scrupulously avoided stimulating drinks such as coffee or tea. However, it turns out that Mormon tea may make you feel slightly stimulated. For generations before the Mormons, the Native Americans of the desert also made a drink from this unassuming plant. Our desert species contains pseudoephedrine, a much weaker form of ephedrine found in species of *Ephedra* found in China and elsewhere. According to Dr. James Adams, California's *Ephedra* plants contain pseudoephedrine, "which is a good nasal decongestant, and a mild stimulant."

I always liked the aroma of the tea, which reminds me of the desert. Plus, if you drink it from a glass, you can observe the tea's subtle pink color.

At home, I just put a small handful of the twigs into a stainless steel pot, add about 2 cups of water, cover, and boil. I let it cook for about 5 minutes and turn off the heat. I pour the water into my cup, sometimes drinking it to alleviate some allergies or minor breathing problems. Though I enjoy the subtle flavor of just the Mormon tea, sometimes I will sweeten it with honey, sometimes with date sugar.

PINE FAMILY (PINACEAE)

The Pine family is said to supply about half the world's lumber needs. The family consists of 10 genera and 193 species.

The Coulter pine, showing needles and cones. LILY JANE TSONG

PINE
Pinus spp.

Use: Needles for tea and spice; nuts for food
Range: Various species are found in the mountains or desert regions; often planted in urban areas.
Similarity to toxic species: None
Best time: Nuts in the fall; needles can be collected anytime.
Status: Common in certain localities
Tools needed: Clippers for needles

Properties
Pines are fairly widespread trees, most commonly found in the higher elevations but also throughout the desert regions (such as the pinyon pine). Not counting subspecies, there are 19 species of *Pinus* in California (94 species in the Northern Hemisphere).

Pines are one of the easier conifers to identify: All the needles are "bundled" at their base into groups of 1 to 5 with papery sheaths called fascicles. Moreover, you will find the fascicle at the base of the needle even when there is only one needle, as in one of the pinyons.

FORAGER NOTE: Some of the very long needles of certain pines are excellent for coiled baskets.

The pines in California can range from short bushes to large, towering trees. To identify a pine tree, look for the bundled needles and the cones. The cones are often whorled with a variety of scale types. As the cones mature, they open up to reveal a pine nut under each scale. Each pine nut has a thin, black shell and a white, oily inside.

Uses

Though there are a few potential foods with the pines, it is mostly the seeds that will provide you with good food. The pinyon pines are arguably the best, and some of the other species have cones that yield flat seeds, or seeds too small to bother with.

The cones mature and open in the fall. As the scales open sufficiently, the seeds drop to the ground, where they can be collected if you're there at the right time and beat the animals to them. The seeds may drop over a 2–4-week period. One of the best methods to harvest them is to lay sheets under the trees to catch the seeds so they're not lost in the grass. The seeds are then shelled and eaten as a snack, added to soups, or mashed and added to biscuits or pancakes.

As some suggest, I have taken the not-fully-mature cones and put them into the fire and carefully watched them so they don't burn. The idea is to open the scales and get the seeds; however, I do not recommend this method. It's too easy to burn the cone, the seeds, and maybe yourself, for seeds that are not really mature.

The tender needles can also be collected and brewed into a tea. Put the needles in a covered container and boil at a low temperature for a few minutes. The tea is rich in vitamin C and very aromatic and tasty—that is, if you enjoy the flavor of a Christmas tree, which is what you'll smell like after drinking it. It's very good.

Yes, we have all heard of eating the cambium layer of pine trees. I once read an article entitled "Spaghetti That Grows on Trees," and it showed a woman who had peeled off the cambium layer of the bark (the inner layer) and had supposedly cooked strips of it to make wild spaghetti. She was actually smiling in the picture, which was my clue that she hadn't actually eaten any of this "spaghetti." I regard this as a "survival food," meaning it is really not worth all the work involved unless you're actually near starving. You most likely would not break into a smile if you were eating such a fibrous and resinous food.

Magnoliids

Magnoliids are terrestrial, containing two cotyledons, with flower parts generally arranged in a spiral or in threes. They are often scented from ethereal oils. Until recently, the group included about 9,000 species, including magnolias, nutmeg, bay laurel, cinnamon, avocado, black pepper, tulip tree, and many others.

Formerly, this was considered a part of the category of Dicots, which are now called Eudicots (see the Eudicots chapter).

LAUREL FAMILY (LAURACEAE)

The Laurel family has 54 genera and approximately 3,500 species worldwide. In California, the family is only represented by the camphor tree (*Cinnamomum camphora*) and the California bay (*Umbellularia californica*).

A view of the leaf and fruit

CALIFORNIA BAY
Umbellularia californica

Use: Leaves for tea and spice; nuts for food
Range: Almost exclusively along streams; sometimes planted in urban areas
Similarity to toxic species: The leaves resemble oleander; however, oleander lacks the strong fragrance of the bay leaf.
Best time: Leaves can be collected anytime; nuts mature in October and November.
Status: Generally restricted to riparian areas
Tools needed: None

California bay nuts

Properties

California bay is primarily a riparian tree, though it can be found as a shrub in the chaparral and occasionally in the urban areas as a landscaping tree.

The leaves are very reminiscent of a lanceolate eucalyptus leaf, except bay leaves are darker and their aroma (especially when crushed) is quite distinctive. The young wood has a darker hue, and the bark becomes smoother and lighter as the plant matures.

The nuts are first green and then they darken before they fall to the ground, somewhat resembling an olive. Once the mushy flesh is removed, there is a thin shell and meat inside.

Uses

Collect the nuts from the ground in the autumn. Remove the flesh and thin shells and dry or roast to make them more palatable. You could also try boiling the shelled nuts. Anthropologist Paul Campbell bakes the bay nuts until they are dark. The flavor is a bit bitter but reminiscent of chocolate!

The nuts could also be dried and ground into flour and used in various pastry products.

The leaves can be used fresh or dried to make a pleasant drink. Add a leaf to your canteen of water, shake it, and enjoy. Or add a leaf to your cup, fill with hot water, and then drink when it's cool enough. It's a delicious tea. The tea is sometimes drunk to relieve stomach pains from overeating or indigestion.

FORAGER NOTE: Though some people have said that their headache was cured by inhaling the fumes from a freshly crushed bay leaf, many others have said that inhaling the strong fragrance causes a headache.

The leaves of this plant have also long been used to repel bugs from bags of rice or beans. This is good practice at home and when traveling. Simply add a few of the dried leaves to a container of rice or other grain. The strong aroma tends to deter the bugs.

Though not a direct food source, archery is one of the ways that indigenous peoples hunted for meat. The long, straight branches of the bay tree provide an excellent material for making long bows.

Cautions

This is not the same leaf as the European bay more typically sold in the spice sections of stores. California bay is much stronger, and some people have a negative reaction (e.g., headaches) to using the leaves for tea. Try just a little at first to make sure you have no reaction.

There are people who have reported headaches after crushing a fresh leaf and holding it close to their nostrils to smell the fragrance. Be cautious even when smelling the leaf.

Eudicots

This category was formerly the bulk of the plants referred to as dicots, that is, plants which begin their growth with 2 cotyledons. (Monocots, by contrast, which include all grasses, begin their growth with a single cotyledon.)

The sprouts begin with 2 cotyledons, and the flower parts are generally in 4s or 5s.

All families in this category are arranged alphabetically by the family's Latin name.

MUSKROOT FAMILY (ADOXACEAE)

This family has 5 genera and about 200 species worldwide. Only 2 of the genera are represented in California.

Elder leaf and flowers

ELDERBERRY
Sambucus spp.

Use: Flowers for tea and food; berries for "raisins," jam, jelly, juice
Range: Elder can be found throughout the state in chaparral, mountains, desert, urban fringes, and, generally, in most environments.
Similarity to toxic species: See Cautions.
Best time: Early spring for flowers; early summer for fruit
Status: Common
Tools needed: Clipper for flowers; clippers and good sturdy basket or bucket for berries

FORAGER NOTE: If you don't want your fruits to get all smashed and crushed, collect them in a basket or bucket (instead of a bag), and don't pack too many into the bucket.

Properties

There are 20 species of *Sambucus* worldwide. According to the latest classification, there are 4 types of elders that you'll find in California: *S. nigra* spp. *caerulea* (blue elderberry), *S. racemosa* (has red or purplish-black fruits), *S. racemosa* var. *melanocarpa* (black elderberry), and *S. racemosa* var. *racemosa* (red elderberry).

Found at higher altitudes, *S. racemosa* var. *melanocarpa* (black elderberry) has purplish-black fruits. *S. nigra* ssp. *caerulea* (formerly *S. mexicana;* Mexican

Elder flower and fruit HELEN W. NYERGES

elder or blue elderberry) is found at lower elevations, throughout the chaparral and below. The fruit is nearly black when ripe, with a white glaucous coating making it appear blue. The *S. racemosa* var. *racemosa* (red elderberry) has red fruits and prefers moist areas.

The different varieties of elder can be found in the dry chaparral regions of California, along streams, and in the higher mountain regions. They are generally small trees with oppositely arranged, pinnately divided leaves with a terminal leaflet. Each leaflet has a fine serration along its edge.

The plant is often inconspicuous in the chaparral but is very obvious when its many yellowish-white flower clusters blossom in the spring.

By early summer, the fruits develop in clusters that often droop from the weight.

RECIPE

Elder Flower Vinegar

Fill a jar with elder flowers (remove as many of the green stems as you can) and then pour in apple cider vinegar or rice vinegar until you reach the top. Close the lid tightly and shake a couple of times daily. Taste after a couple of weeks. Makes a wonderful vinegar with floral flavors.

—RECIPE FROM PASCAL BAUDAR

David Martinez examines the ripe Mexican elder fruit.

Uses

The dark purple berries, rich in vitamin A with fair amounts of potassium and calcium, can be eaten raw (but see Caution section below) or mashed and blended with applesauce for a unique dessert, especially if you are using wild apples. The berries can also be used for making wines, jellies, jams, and pies. (The red berries are not recommended for food because some have toxic qualities.)

Fellow forager and wild food experimenter Pascal Baudar likes to dry and powder the fruit and sprinkle it over ice cream or other dessert items.

The whole flower cluster can be gathered, dipped in batter, and fried, producing a wholesome pancake. Try dipping the flower clusters in a batter of the sweet yellow cattail pollen (see Cattail chapter) and frying them like pancakes. They're delicious!

Another way to use the flowers is to remove them from the clusters and the little stems and then mix with flour in a proportion of 50-50 for baking pastries, breads, biscuits, and more.

The flowers also make a traditional Appalachian tea that was said to be useful for colds, fevers, and headaches.

Elderberry Sauce

This simple sauce goes well with any game (such as duck), but feel free to try it with chicken too!

1 pound elderberries (freeze the clusters first, crush them lightly with your hands, and the berries will fall easily)

1 large sweet onion or 7–8 scallions

⅔ cup red wine vinegar

¾ cup sugar or honey

1 teaspoon grated ginger

A couple of cloves

½ teaspoon salt, or to taste

Place the berries in a pot and first squeeze them with your hand to release the juice. Add the remaining ingredients and bring to a boil for 10 minutes. Strain the liquid through a sieve.

Return the liquid to the pot, bring to a simmer, and reduce until you have achieved the right consistency (like a commercial steak sauce). You can prepare it in advance and keep it in the fridge for many days.

—RECIPE FROM PASCAL BAUDAR

The long, straight stems of elder have a soft pith, and they have historically been hollowed-out and used for such things as pipe stems, blowguns, flutes, and straws for stoking a fire.

Cautions

Be sure to cook the fruit before eating it, and avoid the red berries entirely. While not everyone will get sick from eating the dark purple or black berries raw, they can cause severe nausea in some people. Therefore, cook all fruit before using for drinks or other dishes.

Do not consume the leaves, as this will result in sickness.

FIG MARIGOLD FAMILY (AIZOACEAE)

This family has 130 genera and approximately 2,500 species worldwide. Eleven genera are found in California.

Young New Zealand spinach

NEW ZEALAND SPINACH
Tetragonia tetragonioides

Use: Leaves cooked or raw
Range: Along the beaches; also easily cultivated
Similarity to toxic species: None
Best time: Though you could collect the greens year-round, the ideal time is spring and early summer when the new growth is coming out.
Status: Generally found in scattered patches
Tools needed: None

Properties
Though there are 50 species worldwide of *Tetragonia*, this is the only species that you'll find in California. It is not a native but comes from the Southern Hemisphere.

After the rain, New Zealand spinach

In the wild, you will find New Zealand spinach along the Pacific Coast in the sand, mostly in sandy dunes. These beach plants often grow beyond the high-tide line. The alternate leaves are fleshy and succulent and resemble common spinach or lamb's quarter, though the plant is weak stemmed and sprawls in the sand, rarely rising more than a few inches off the ground. The individual leaves are rarely more than 2" long.

There are sessile flowers, but they are inconspicuous. The little nutlike seeds fall on the ground around the plant. These can be collected for propagation.

Because the plant is easily cultivated, it can also be found in yards and old gardens throughout the state. The plant survives fairly well even when left alone, assuming the soil is at least of average richness, with some shade and some moisture.

Uses

New Zealand spinach is one of those highly versatile plants with mild-tasting leaves that can be

FORAGER NOTE: If you allow the New Zealand spinach to grow in your garden, it will produce spinach greens forever. To harvest it, just pinch off the new growth.

New Zealand spinach being prepared for soup. HELEN W. NYERGES

used in a broad selection of dishes. Think of it as a perennial spinach with leaves more succulent than regular spinach. The leaves are a bit stronger than regular spinach, though most people will even enjoy it as a trail nibble.

The tender leaves are great in a simple salad or mixed with other greens. They can be used in stir-fries and soup dishes and cooked with eggs. If you try cooking the leaves similar to spinach, try drinking the water. It's a tasty broth and can be used as the basis for a soup stock.

If you don't live right on the coast, you can still get the seeds or live plants (from a nursery) and grow this in your self-sufficiency garden. Unlike regular spinach, the New Zealand spinach is a perennial that grows and spreads and reseeds itself. If you're someone who wants a food-producing garden that more or less takes care of itself, this is the plant to have. Plant it once, take care of it, and have food for decades.

RECIPE

The Moon Sets in the Malibu Lagoon

Finely chop 1 cup of New Zealand spinach leaves. Add 1 tablespoon tuna fish. Top with an oil-and-vinegar dressing to taste.

AMARANTH FAMILY (AMARANTHACEAE)

The Amaranth family has 75 genera and approximately 900 species worldwide, with 4 genera in California.

One of the erect amaranths

AMARANTH
Amaranthus spp.

Use: Seeds for soup or pastry and bread products; leaf can be used raw or cooked.

Range: Amaranth is widespread. Though it is most common in the disturbed soils of farms, gardens, fields, and urban lots, you can usually find some amaranth in the deserts and in open areas where there is some moisture, even if that moisture is seasonal.

Similarity to toxic species: Some ornamentals resemble amaranth. Some toxic plants superficially resemble the amaranth plants. Individual jimsonweed leaves have been confused with amaranth leaves. Generally, once the amaranth begins to flower and go to seed, this confusion is diminished.

Best time: Spring is best for the leaves; late fall for the seeds.

Status: Common

Tools needed: You'll need a tight-weave bag for collecting the seeds.

Properties

There are 13 species of *Amaranthus* in California; 7 are native.

Amaranth is an annual. The ones with erect stalks can grow to 3' and taller, depending on the species. Some are more branched and lower to the ground. When young, the root of one of the common varieties, *A. retroflexus,* is red, and the bottoms of the leaves are purple. The leaves of *A. retroflexus* are oval shaped, alternate, and glossy. Other *Amaranthus* leaves can be ovate to linear.

The plant produces flowers, but they are not conspicuous. They are formed in spikelike clusters, and numerous shiny black seeds develop when the plant matures in late summer. The plant is common and widespread in urban areas, fields, farms, backyards, and roadsides.

A. retroflexus. Note the red root. RICK ADAMS

Uses

Amaranth is a versatile plant with edible parts available throughout its growing season.

The young leaves and tender stems of late winter and spring can be eaten raw in salads; however, because there is often a hint of bitterness, they are best mixed with other greens. Young and tender stems are boiled in many parts of the world and served with butter or cheese as a simple vegetable. Older leaves get bitter and should be boiled into a spinach-like dish or added to dishes such as soups, stews, and stir-fries.

In Mexico, leaves are sometimes dried and made into a flour, which is added to tamales and other dishes.

FORAGER NOTE: Amaranths are a diverse group: Some have an erect stalk, some are highly branched, and some are prostrate.

Amaranth begins to produce seeds in late summer, and once the seeds are black, they can be harvested. Generally, the entire plant is very withered and dried-up by the time you're harvesting. The seeds are added to soups, bread batter, and pastry products. Ground-up seeds sweetened with honey are used to make a traditional Mexican *atole.*

A. retroflexus leaves RICK ADAMS

The seed and leaf are very nutritious, no doubt part of the reason this plant was so revered in the old days. Consider this: 100 g of the seed contains about 358 calories, 247 mg of calcium, 500 mg of phosphorus, and 52.5 mg of potassium. The seed offers a nearly complete balance of essential amino acids, including lysine and methionine.

The leaf is also very nutritious, being high in calcium and potassium: 100 g, which is about ½ cup, of amaranth leaf has 267–448 mg of calcium, 411–617 mg of potassium, 53–80 mg of vitamin C, 4,300 mcg (micrograms) of beta carotene, and 1,300 mcg of niacin. This volume of leaf contains about 35 calories.

Historical note: The seed and leaf of this plant played a key part of the diet in precolonial Mexico. The seeds were mixed with honey or blood and shaped into images of their gods, and these images were then eaten as a communion. Sound familiar? After the Spanish invaded Mexico, they made it illegal to grow the amaranth plant, with the justification that it was a part of "pagan rituals."

CARROT FAMILY (APIACEAE)

The Carrot family has about 300 genera worldwide, with about 3,000 species. In California, there are 39 genera of this family. Many are cultivated for food, spice, and medicine, but some are highly toxic. Never eat anything that looks like carrot or parsley if you haven't positively identified it.

Young fennel plant

FENNEL
Foeniculum vulgare

Use: Leaf and stalk raw or cooked; seed for tea or seasoning
Range: Widespread as an invasive species along the coast; common locally in urban lots and fields
Similarity to toxic species: Fennel has needlelike leaves and smells like licorice, so you really shouldn't confuse it with anything toxic. However, this family contains some poisonous and toxic members, so be certain you're picking fennel before eating it.
Best time: Spring is best for the young shoots; collect the seeds in summer or fall.
Status: Widespread and common in certain localities
Tools needed: None

Nathaniel Schleimer examines fennel plants. HELEN W. NYERGES

Properties

Fennel is the only species of the *Foeniculum* genus.

Fennel is a perennial from Europe that is very common along the Pacific Coast and in wet areas. It is very abundant in certain places and generally considered invasive.

The plant begins to produce its leaves in the spring. The finely dissected leaves give the plant a ferny appearance. The base of each leaf clasps the stalk with a flared base, similar to the base of a celery stalk. The unmistakable characteristic is the strong licorice aroma of the crushed leaf.

In winter and early spring, the plants begin to appear. They first establish a ferny, bushy 2'–3' broad base. By spring and early summer, the flower stalks rise to a height of 6' (higher in ideal conditions). The entire plant has a slightly bluish-green cast due to a thin, waxy coating on the stalks and leaves.

The yellow flowers form in large, distinctive umbels.

Uses

Young fennel leaves and peeled stalks are great to eat as a trail snack when you're thirsty and hungry. When the plant first sprouts up in the spring, you can eat the entire tender, succulent base of the plant, somewhat like you'd eat celery. As it sends up its stalk but before the plant has flowered, the stalk is still tender and can be easily cut into segments. These tender segments are hollow and round in the cross section and can be used like celery for dipping or cooked similar to asparagus and served with cheese and butter.

Later, as the plant grows taller, you can eat the tender leaves and stems chopped up in salads or added to soups and stews. It gets a bit fibrous as it matures, but it can be diced up and added to many dishes. It adds a sweet spiciness to the dishes in which it is used. If you don't care for licorice, you probably won't care for fennel.

When the seeds mature, they can be made into a licorice-flavored tea. Just put 5 or 6 seeds into a cup and add hot water.

The seeds alone can be chewed as a breath freshener or used to season other dishes.

Fennel is widely considered a pest in California because, in some areas, it grows so thick that it will choke out native vegetation. However, this is one of those ideal plants to grow in a lazy person's garden. It seems to take care of itself, does well in sun or shade, and continues to arise from its roots year after year.

SUNFLOWER FAMILY (ASTERACEAE)

Worldwide, the Sunflower family has about 1,500 genera and about 23,000 species! This is the largest family in California. *Jepson* divides this very large family into 14 groups. All plants addressed here from the Sunflower family are within Group 8, described as having ligulate heads, 5-lobed ligules (5 teeth per petal), and, generally, containing milky sap when broken. When I began studying botany in the 1970s, my teachers described this group as the Chicory Tribe, a much more descriptive title than the unimaginative "Group 8." According to Dr. Leonid Enari, the Chicory Tribe contains no poisonous members and is a worthy group for further edibility research. I have eaten many of the other members of this group not listed here, though generally they require extensive boiling and water changing to render them edible and palatable.

The overall chicory plants RICK ADAMS

CHICORY
Cichorium intybus

Use: Root for beverage and food; greens raw or cooked
Range: Widespread, more so in the northern part of the state; especially found in the disturbed soils of farms, fields, and gardens
Similarity to toxic species: None

Best time: Spring is ideal for collecting.
Status: Common locally
Tools needed: Tool for digging roots

Properties

There are 6 species worldwide in the *Cichorium* genus. Chicory is one of only 2 species of *Cichorium* in California; the other is endive, which is not common and is typically found near gardens or farms where it goes wild.

The chicory plant grows upright 3'–5' tall and typically with prominent sky-blue flowers. Look carefully at the flower—the tip of each petal is divided into 5 teeth, typical of the Chicory Tribe of the Sunflower family. Each leaf will produce a bit of milky sap when cut. The older upper leaves on the stalk very characteristically clasp the stem at the base. This is a perennial from Europe that is now widespread in parts of California, mostly the north. It is found in fields, along roadsides, in gardens, on farms, and in disturbed soils.

Chicory flower RICK ADAMS

A view of the leaf RICK ADAMS

Uses

This is another of those incredibly nutritious plants with multiple uses. The leaves, preferably the very young leaves, can be added to salads; if you don't mind a bit of bitter, the older leaves can be added. The leaves can be cooked similar to spinach and added to a variety of dishes, such as soups, stews, and egg dishes.

Chicory roots are also used whole or sliced, either boiled and buttered or added to stews and soups. Roots in rich soil tend to be less woody and fibrous.

Chicory roots have long been used as a substitute for coffee or as a coffee extender. Dig and wash the roots, and then dry them, grind them, and roast them until they are brown. Now use them alone, just as you'd use regular coffee grounds, or you can add them to coffee as an extender.

Incidentally, you can make this same coffee substitute or extender with the roots of dandelion and sow thistle.

Note: The entire Chicory Tribe of the Sunflower family contains no poisonous members, though many are bitter. These are, generally, tender-leafed plants with milky sap and with dandelion-like flowers, each petal of which usually has 5 teeth at the tip.

Prickly lettuce (sow thistle to right)

PRICKLY LETTUCE
Lactuca serriola and others

Use: Young leaves raw or cooked
Range: Most commonly found in gardens, disturbed soils, along trails, edges of farms
Similarity to toxic species: None
Best time: Early spring
Status: Widespread
Tools needed: None

Properties
Though there are about 100 species of *Lactuca* worldwide, we have only 7 species in California, and only 2 are native (*L. tatarica* and *L. biennis*). *L. serriola*, a European native, is probably the most abundant and widespread.

Young rosette of prickly lettuce, still OK in salads

Prickly lettuce is actually a very common annual plant that you can find just about anywhere, hidden in plain view. Yes, you've seen it, but it likely blended into the landscape. It's mostly an urban "weed," though occasionally you'll find it in the near wilderness surrounding urban areas. It's originally from Europe.

Prickly lettuce rises with its erect stalk to typically no more than 3'. The young leaves are lanceolate with generally rounded ends. They are tender; if you tear a leaf, you'll see white sap. The plant grows upright with a straight stem that develops soft spines as it gets older. As the plant matures, you'll note that there is a stiff line of hairs on the bottom midrib of the leaf. The leaf attachment is either sessile or clasping the stem. Moreover, the leaf shape can be quite variable, from a simple oblong lanceolate leaf to one that is divided into pinnately lobed segments. Despite this, after you've seen a few prickly lettuce plants, you should readily recognize it.

The flowers are small and dandelion-like, pale yellow, with about a dozen ray flowers per head. As with dandelion, these mature into small seeds attached to a little cottony tuft.

FORAGER NOTE: One of the common names for this plant is compass plant. When the plant is mature, the edges of the leaves tend to point to the sun as it moves across the sky. This is probably a mechanism to stop water loss. While this is by no means as accurate as using a compass, it could help you generally determine directions with a bit of figuring.

Uses

Prickly lettuce sounds like something you'd really like in a salad, but in fact, you need to find the very youngest leaves for salad, or they get too tough and bitter. Very young leaves (before the plant has sent up its flower stalk) are good added to your salads and sandwiches.

The leaves can also be collected and mixed into stir-fries or added to soups and any sort of stew in which you can add wild greens.

However, let's not be fooled by the name "lettuce." Yes, it's botanically a relative of the cultivar you buy at the supermarket, but the leaves get significantly bitter as they age. Moreover, the rib on the underside of each older leaf develops these stiff spines that make any similarity to lettuce very distant. This means you'll be using this plant raw only when it's very young; and when it's flowering and mature, you probably won't be using it at all.

Still, it's food, it's edible, and it grows everywhere. You should get to know this plant and its relatives and learn to recognize it early in the growing season.

I've used it when *very* young in sandwiches, salads, soups, stews, and egg dishes. I've even used the small root when I was experimenting with coffee substitutes. Because this is related to dandelion and sow thistle, I figured it would work well as a coffee substitute, and it does, but there's very little root to this plant.

Sow thistle in flower

SOW THISTLE
Sonchus oleraceus and others

Use: Mostly the leaves, raw or cooked; root cooked and eaten; flower buds pickled
Range: Most common in urban areas, gardens, and farms, but also found in most environments
Similarity to toxic species: None
Best time: Spring is best, though the older leaves of late summer are still useful.
Status: Common
Tools needed: Trowel for digging

Properties
There are 55 known species of *Sonchus* worldwide. Four of these species are found in California, and all are originally from Europe. Though the common sow thistle (*S. oleraceus*) is most often used for food, the other 3 look very similar and can be used likewise. However, when you see *S. asper*, the prickly sow thistle,

you may conclude that it's too much work to use for a dish of cooked greens because it is covered with soft spines.

When most people see a flowering common sow thistle for the first time, they think it's a dandelion. Well, it is related to the dandelion, and yes, the flowers are very similar. However, here is a simple distinction: All dandelion leaves arise directly from the taproot, forming a basal rosette. Sow thistle sends up a much taller stalk, up to 5' or so in ideal conditions, but usually about 3'. The leaves are formed along this more-or-less erect and branching stalk. The leaves are paler and more tender than dandelion leaves, and

Sow thistle in flower

sow thistle leaves are not as jagged on the edges as dandelion. And though the individual dandelion and sow thistle flowers are very similar, dandelion only forms one flower per stalk, whereas sow thistle will form many flowers per stalk.

Uses

Though sow thistle may not be quite as nutritious as dandelion, it's definitely tastier, and the leaves are more tender. You can take the leaves of sow thistle and include them in salads; and even when the plant is old, there is only a hint of bitterness. The flavor and texture are very much like lettuce that you might grow in your garden.

The leaves and tender stems are also ideally added to soups and stews or simply cooked by themselves and served similar to spinach greens. They are tasty on their own, or you can try different seasonings (peppers, butter, cheese, etc.) that you enjoy.

The root can be eaten or made into a coffee substitute, as is commonly

FORAGER NOTE: Sow thistle is one of our most common wild foods. It is so widespread that it can be found in nearly every environment, even in the cracks of urban sidewalks.

Spring Awakening

For a dish that resembles asparagus, take the tender sow thistle stems in the spring-time (the leaves can be removed and added to other dishes). Boil or steam them until tender—it doesn't take long—and then lay the stems on your plate like asparagus. Add some cheese or butter, and it will make a delicious dish. However, this is a dish that you'll only enjoy in the spring—timing is everything.

done with two of its relatives, dandelion and chicory. To eat the roots, gather the young ones and boil until tender. Season as you wish and serve. The roots could also be washed and added to soups and stews.

For a coffee substitute, gather and wash the roots and then dry thoroughly. Grind them into a coarse meal, roast to a light shade of brown, and then percolate into a caffeine-free beverage. Is it good? It's all a matter of personal preference.

Dandelion rosette and seeding flower heads

DANDELION
Taraxacum officinale

Use: Leaves raw or cooked; root cooked or processed into a beverage
Range: Prefers lawns, fields, and disturbed soils
Similarity to toxic species: None
Best time: Spring for the greens; anytime for the roots
Status: Common
Tools needed: Trowel for the roots

Dandelion rosette

Properties

The *Taraxacum* genus has 60 species worldwide. In California, there are 4 species of *Taraxacum;* 2 are native, and 2 are from Europe. The common dandelion (*T. officinale*) is from Europe. California dandelion (*T. californicum*) and horned dandelion (*T. ceratophorum*) are our native dandelions.

Even people who say they don't know how to identify any plants can probably identify a dandelion in a field. The characteristic yellow composite flower sits atop the narrow stem, which arises directly from the taproot. There is one yellow flower per flower stalk. These mature into the round, puffy seed heads that children enjoy blowing on to make a wish.

These grow in fields, in lawns, in vacant lots, and along trails. They tend to prefer disturbed soils, though I have seen them in the wilderness.

The leaves are dark green, toothed on the margins, and each arises from the root. The name "dandelion" actually comes from the French *dent de leon,* meaning "tooth of the lion," for the jagged edges of the leaves.

Uses

My first exposure to dandelion was at about age 7 when my father would pay me a nickel to dig them out of our front-yard lawn and throw them into the trash.

Boy, things have changed! These days, I would not consider having a front lawn, and I definitely would not dig out the dandelions and toss them in the trash.

Dandelion is another versatile wild food. The yellow flowers make the plant conspicuous in field and lawns, though it's really the leaves and root that are most used by the forager.

Young leaves are the best, and because they are bitter, they are usually blanched before eating. They can be used in any cooked dish where you'd add greens, such as soups, stews, and omelets.

If you want raw dandelion greens, you'll want to pick them as early as possible in the season or they become bitter. Bitter is not bad, and it can be mellowed out by adding other greens. Also, oil-rich dressing makes a dandelion salad more palatable.

It's understandable that dandelions have gotten more popular—they are, after all, the richest source of beta carotene, even more so than carrots. However, not all the greens sold as dandelions at farmers' markets and supermarkets are the genuine leaf. Frequently, we will see various endive relatives sold and called "dandelion."

The roots are also edible. The younger roots, and plants growing in rich soil, are more tender and more desirable. However, I have eaten old roots and tough roots and have found a way to make them more palatable: Generally, I scrub the roots to get rid of all the soil and then boil them until tender. You can boil them whole or slice them, and when tender, you can use them in stews and soups.

For a coffee-substitute beverage, wash and dry the roots. Though there are a few ways you can do this, I generally do a coarse grind and then roast them in the oven until they are light brown. Then I do a fine grind and percolate them into a beverage. You can drink it black or you can add honey and cream.

Oh yes, and then there's dandelion wine …

These days, I can't think of dandelions without thinking of Dr. Peter Gail of Cleveland, Ohio, who spent his life promoting wild foods in general and dandelions in particular. He led workshops, seminars, and cookouts to promote the many uses of dandelion, and he compiled recipes in his popular *Dandelion Celebration* book, a collection of everything you'd ever want to know about dandelions.

MUSTARD FAMILY (BRASSICACEAE)

The Mustard family is another large family, comprising more than 330 genera worldwide and about 3,780 species. In California, the Mustard family is represented by 64 genera.

The floral characteristics that define the Mustard family are 4 free petals, 4 sepals (generally white or yellow but other colors as well), 6 stamens (4 long, 2 short), 1 pistil, a superior ovary, and fruits that are generally a capsule or silique with 2 valves. Many are cultivated for foods and some for ornamentals. *The Jepson Manual* divides this family into 8 groups. Dr. Leonid Enari stated that he was unaware of any toxic member of this group, though some are more palatable than others. As a result, I have experimented with many of the Mustard family species in various parts of North and Central America.

Young *Brassica*

MUSTARD
Brassica spp. (including *Hirschfeldia incana*, "Mediterranean mustard," formerly known as *B. geniculata*)

Use: Leaves raw or cooked; seeds for spice; flowers for garnish

Range: Fields, urban areas, and chaparral hillsides

Similarity to toxic species: None

Best time: Spring for greens and flowers

Status: Widespread

Tools needed: None

Properties

There are 35 species of *Brassica* worldwide. Seven of those genera, all non-natives, can be found in California.

Though you should learn to recognize the common mustards even when the plant is not in flower, it is the flower that will initially draw you to the plant. The bright yellow flower has the typical Mustard family flora arrangement: 4 petals (shaped in an X or cross), 4 sepals (1 under each petal), 4 stamens, and 1 pistil. These are formed in a raceme with the buds toward the tops, then the mature flowers, and then, lower

Mustard flowers HELEN W. NYERGES

on the stalk, the seedpods form. The needle-thin seedpods are about 1" long.

The initial basal leaves are lyrately-pinnately divided, meaning that they have the appearance of a guitar with a large, round lateral lobe and smaller side lobes. Not exactly like a guitar, but it gives you a good mental picture. As the plant matures, the leaves that form on the upper stalks are smaller and linear and look nothing like the young basal leaves.

Uses

Mustard is one of the first wild foods that I began to eat, partly because it is so common and partly because it is so easy to identify. I recall seeing a line drawing of it in Bradford Angier's *Free for the Eating*, which didn't look anything like the green plant with yellow flowers that I was seeing all over Southern California. Angier used a picture of the mature plant gone to seed, and what I was seeing was the young spring plant. They were both right, but it demonstrated the need to always learn plants by seeing them in the field.

I began with the young mustard greens, chewing the raw leaves and enjoying the spicy flavor, despite the fine hairs covering the leaves (not all *Brassicas* are hairy). I then moved on to chopping them up and adding them to salads, which was good. I then began to boil the leaves and serve to my family with butter. Everyone enjoyed it, even my father.

FORAGER NOTE: This is a hardy plant. I have managed to find some mustard greens even during droughts when no other greens are available.

Mustard leaves and stems

Eventually, I found that I could add mustard greens to just about any dish: soups, mixed salads, omelets, stir-fries, potatoes, you name it! The fact that I could collect these greens year-round in California was also a big plus.

The flower buds and flowers have also been a good trail treat, and they make a good, colorful garnish to salads and soups. I give them to children and tell them that they taste similar to broccoli, and most of the children say they enjoy the flowers.

The tender tops of the stems with the flower buds can also be snapped off the upper parts of the plant, steamed, and served with some sauce or cheese. The flavor is similar to the Chinese broccoli that you buy at farmers' markets.

Lastly, you can come back to this annual plant in late fall, when the leaves are dried up and the tops are just tan-colored stems with small seedpods. Collect the pods in a bag (a pillowcase is ideal), and break them all up. The seeds go to the bottom of the bag, and you can discard the pod shell. The seeds are then used as a seasoning for various dishes calling for mustard, or you can try making your own mustard condiment from the brown seeds.

RECIPE

Pascal's Mustard

Fellow forager Pascal Baudar takes the pungent flowers of regular black mustard and grinds them while fresh, adding white wine and vinegar to taste. Thus, he produces a mustard condiment from the flowers, not the seed as is the usual custom.

A view of the overall plant RICK ADAMS

SEA ROCKET
Cakile edentula and *C. maritima*

Use: Greens, sprouts, and flowers are ideally cooked but can be used raw sparingly.
Range: Restricted to the sandy beaches along the entire California coast
Similarity to toxic species: None
Best time: Spring, but can be picked year-round
Status: Somewhat common
Tools needed: None

Properties
There are 7 species of *Cakile* worldwide, found on the beach shores of North America, Africa, and Europe. On California's west coast, we have 2 species of *Cakile,* both introduced.

In California, sea rocket is widespread along the coast, growing in the sand in the upper areas of the beach, usually just beyond high tide in the dunes. When you see how well these plants have naturalized, it is hard to believe that they are not natives. *C. maritima* is the one that you most commonly see on California beaches, and it is native to Europe. *C. edentula* is also found on beaches and is native to the East Coast of the United States. The leaves are very much like a small mustard leaf, but they are plump, as if swollen. Each leaf has a bluish-green appearance, with the leaves pinnately divided into linear segments. Typically, each leaf tends to fold inward along the central vein of the leaf.

The seedpods also look swollen, and you can see why the plant is called "rocket" by looking at the pod's space rocket–like appearance.

Of course, the lavender to light purple flower has the typical mustard flower arrangement of 4 petals, 4 sepals, 6 stamens, and 1 pistil.

Uses

The leaves are strongly flavored similar to horseradish, and generally you would not want to include the mature leaves in a salad. However, boiling tones them down quite a bit so they are tastier and more palatable. The boiled leaves can be added for flavor to soup broths or to dishes

A view of sea rocket's seedpods RICK ADAMS

of mixed greens. In general, you'd probably not want to serve them alone as a cooked green unless you changed the water once and served them with some onions and probably a savory sauce.

Still, they can turn an otherwise bland meal into quite a treat. They will help to flavor clam chowder as well as other soups and stews. They will really liven up stale old MREs.

RECIPE

We have finely diced the sea rocket leaves into nearly a paste and mixed in a very small amount of oil and vinegar, creating a passable "wasabi."

The beautiful lavender flower of sea rocket RICK ADAMS

Once, while camping on the coast north of San Francisco, we were hiking in the sand above the high-tide line. It was very foggy in the wintertime, and most of the sea rocket was dried and gone to seed. Under one very large, old, bushy sea rocket plant, we noticed hundreds of little sprouts in the sand. We carefully harvested many of these. Each was tender and not at all harshly flavored, as the more mature plant tends to be. We added some to salad for our mostly foraged meal that evening, and the rest we added to our homemade clam chowder.

Think of sea rocket more as a flavoring agent and garnish, not as a principal food.

Young sea rocket leaves RICK ADAMS

Indian cabbage in the field OTTO GASSER, SAN EMIGDIO MOUNTAINS REGION OF CALIFORNIA

INDIAN CABBAGE
Calanthus inflatus

Use: Greens and top buds, cooked
Range: Restricted to the Mojave Desert and its fringes
Similarity to toxic species: None
Best time: Spring, after a wet winter
Status: Appears in the open areas single or in groups; some years, it will not appear if there are insufficient rains.
Tools needed: None

Properties
There are 17 species of *Calanthus* in the Southwest and Mexico. In California, we find 16 species, all native.

Indian cabbage, also called desert candle, is a distinctive plant when you encounter it in the open, sandy areas of the desert and in the dry hillsides. Most often, you will find it in the Mojave Desert in the spring after a winter of average to above-average rain. In years of drought, you will not see this plant.

The most notable feature is the erect and inflated stem, which rises up about 1.5' (or so). The flower tips are dark purple, white at the base. This is the only species of *Calanthus* where the stigma is purplish. The overall effect when you look at the flowering plant is of a candle, burning at the top. (OK, so you need to have *some* imagination!) The leaves form in a basal rosette, and they somewhat have the texture of cabbage (though not the shape). The bases of the upper leaves are strongly lobed and clasping the stem.

Uses

The desert Indians were known to have used the leaves and tender stems for food. I have nibbled the young leaves and, though they were certainly edible, they were not ideal for salads unless they were collected when they were very young in the year.

The flavor is improved by cooking. I have added the younger leaves to cooked soups and stews and

Indian cabbage flower OTTO GASSER, SAN EMIGDIO MOUNTAINS REGION OF CALIFORNIA

found them delicious, though some of my camping partners said the leaves were just "tolerable." The leaves should be rinsed of sand, diced, and then cooked with egg dishes, stir-fries, and other vegetable dishes.

Both the leaves and the tip of the flower stalk can be used.

FORAGER NOTE: My first encounters with this annual plant were in the winter when the plant had died and left a hollow stalk. When the wind came through and blew across the hollow tubes, it created an eerie music of the desert.

A patch of flowering Indian cabbage OTTO GASSER, SAN EMIGDIO MOUNTAINS REGION
OF CALIFORNIA

Though this may seem like a marginal food, you should keep in mind that
food is not always very common or widespread in the desert. It's good to know
as many foods from the desert as possible. Moreover, with this one, timing is
everything. You will find the plant in the greatest abundance after a wet winter
and spring. Then, once the heat of summer is upon us, the plants quickly dry up
and disappear. In some seasons, you may not see any of this plant at all.

If you choose to try a few of these leaves during a spring desert campout,
remember only to pick the few leaves that you need, and don't uproot the plant!

Shepherd's purse, in seed, arising from a field of chickweed

SHEPHERD'S PURSE
Capsella bursa-pastoris

Use: Leaves used raw or cooked; medicine
Range: Prefers lawns, fields, disturbed soils, lower chaparral zone
Similarity to toxic species: None
Best time: Spring is best for greens; the seed can be collected in late spring to early summer.
Status: Somewhat common
Tools needed: None

Properties

There are 4 species of *Capsella* worldwide, and only *C. bursa-pastoris* is found in California.

Shepherd's purse is most easily identified by its flat, heart-shaped seedpods. They are unmistakable! The stalks rise about 1' or so tall. The little clusters of white flowers, sometimes tinged with a bit of purple, are formed in racemes along the stalk. These mature into the heart-shaped pods. Trouble is, by the time you see all the seedpods, it's usually too late to use the young leaves for food, but at least now you know how to recognize shepherd's purse.

The young leaves are often hidden in the grass and are somewhat inconspicuous. The basal leaves are toothed, with a large terminal lobe, typical of Mustard family leaves. The upper leaves are without a stalk and are more arrowhead shaped. If you look closely, the young leaves will be covered with little hairs.

Uses

The flavor of shepherd's purse leaves are mild, and they could be used in just about any recipe, such as salads, sandwiches, soup, eggs, and so on. However, they seem best when used in salads.

Dr. Enari used to poll his students on which plant tasted the best of the many wild plants he let them try. Consistently in his polls, shepherd's purse was rated the best. It is actually somewhat bland and peppery but not *too* peppery, and the texture is mild. Even finicky eaters will like these leaves.

Heart-shaped seedpods of shepherd's purse

It's also very nutritious. About a half cup of the leaves (100 g) contains 208 mg of calcium, 86 mg of phosphorus, 40 mg of sodium, 394 mg of potassium, 36 mg of vitamin C, and 1,554 international units (IUs) of vitamin A.

Additionally, some Native Americans ground the seed into a meal and used it in drinks and as flour for various dishes.

Dr. Enari told his students that this was the best plant to stop nosebleeds. Boil the plant, put a cotton ball into the water, and then apply it to the nose. It turns out that many people have used this plant medicinally, especially to stop internal or external bleeding.

Young shepherd's purse

Watercress

WATERCRESS
Nasturtium officinale

Use: Leaves raw or cooked in salads, stir-fries, soup, and so on; can be dried for use as a seasoning
Range: Restricted to the edges of lakes and streams
Similarity to toxic species: None! However, in one case of death by poison hemlock, two campers in the Santa Cruz area cooked and ate the plant. Both became sick quickly, and one managed to walk and get help; the other camper was found dead when rescuers returned. The survivor said that they thought the plant they ate was watercress. Though watercress and poison hemlock can grow in the same wet areas, they are very different-looking plants. Never eat any plant until you have made a positive identification.
Best time: Although the plant can be collected at any time, it's best in spring before the plant flowers.
Status: Somewhat common along streams
Tools needed: None

Properties
There are 5 species of *Nasturtium* worldwide. Two of these species are found in California, and both are considered natives.

Once you learn to recognize watercress and see how the pinnately divided leaves are formed, you will find it quite easy to recognize, whether it is very young or older and flowering.

First, it nearly always grows directly on the edges of streams where water is slower. Occasionally, you'll find it in sandy areas, but it is always in an area that is at least seasonally underwater. You'll typically find it growing in thick mats.

The leaves are pinnately divided into round leaflets. The stems are hollow, and there are white hairs on the underwater part of the stem.

The plant is in the Mustard family; when it gets older and flowers, the white flowers will be divided into the typical Mustard family formula: 4 petals, 4 sepals, 6 stamens, and 1 pistil.

Though watercress can today be found worldwide, it is regarded by botanists as a native plant in California. It was known to be a part of the diet of early Native Americans.

Uses

Watercress was one of the very first wild plants that I learned how to identify and began to use. It is not only common throughout waterways (streams and ditches) in California but also throughout the world.

I have always enjoyed making a salad of mixed greens and including watercress. However, I don't usually make a salad with *only* watercress because it's a bit too spicy for my taste. A few raw watercress leaves are also tasty in sandwiches.

For soup, just chop the entire plant (tender stems and leaves) fine and add it to a water- or milk-based soup. Or you can add chopped watercress leaves to a miso base. Watercress makes a delicious soup.

Watercress in flower HELEN W. NYERGES

You can cook the greens similar to spinach, serving it with a simple seasoning such as butter or cheese. Alternatively, try mixing the greens into an omelet.

If you're living off MREs or freeze-dried camping food, you can add some diced watercress to liven up your meals.

Also, for those of you who'd like making your own spices, you can dry and powder watercress and use it to season various dishes. Use it alone or blend the powdered watercress with powdered seaweed or other flavorful herbs. You'll notice that some of the commercial salt-alternative spices use dried watercress leaves.

Another self-reliant idea is to dry wild foods into the basis of a soup stock and then reconstitute them later into a soup or stew

Christopher collecting watercress BARBARA KOLANDER

broth. Dried and powdered watercress makes an ideal ingredient in such a mix.

Cautions

If you have doubts about the purity of the water where you get your watercress, you should not eat it raw. Instead, boil it first and then use it in a cooked dish.

Always wash watercress before using. It grows right in the water, and you want to remove any dirt or other undesirables that may be clinging to the plant.

RECIPE

Saturday Night Special

Gently sauté half an onion bulb, minced, in a skillet with butter; you could substitute a handful of wild or garden onion greens. Quickly, add at least 1 cup chopped watercress leaves and stems and cook gently until all is tender. Add a dash of soy sauce and serve.

Young radish leaf. Note red in stem.

WILD RADISH
Raphanus sativus and *R. raphanistrum*

Use: All tender portions of this plant—leaf, stems, pods, flowers—can be used raw, pickled, or cooked. Roots generally are not used.
Range: Fields, wet areas, farmlands, vacant lots, disturbed soils
Similarity to toxic species: None
Best time: Spring into summer is best
Status: Common
Tools needed: Clippers

Properties
There are 3 species of *Raphanus*. Two are found in California, and both are natives of the Mediterranean area.

Each young leaf of wild radish is lyrately-pinnately divided, meaning that there are both 1 large end lobe and smaller side lobes or segments to the leaf: It resembles a guitar! When the young leaves of wild radish are newly emerging, it would be easy to confuse the leaves with those of mustard (*Brassica* spp.). However, wild radish leaf lacks the fine hairs that you find on mustard. If you examine a wild radish leaf closely, it will be covered somewhat sparsely with bristles, the leaf surface will be smoother than mustard, and you will see a tinge of red in the midrib of the radish leaf.

As the plant flowers, instead of the usual yellow mustard flowers, the flowers will be lavender or white or, very rarely, pale yellow. There is the typical Mustard family flower formula of 4 petals, 4 sepals, 6 stamens (4 long and 2 short), and 1 pistil. The flowers are followed by fleshy seedpods that resemble pointed jalapeño peppers.

The root of wild radish is a white taproot, not at all like the radish you might grow in your garden or buy in the store. It is largely woody and inedible, though there

Radish flower and bud

is a soft outer layer that can be peeled off. The taste of this outer root layer is so obviously "radish" that most anyone can identify this plant by the aroma and flavor. Though the root is nearly always a white taproot, we've found at least a few that were large and round when growing in thick mulch during a wet season.

Overall, the wild radish plant can grow up to 4', and it can be even taller in ideal conditions.

Radish pods RICK ADAMS

Uses

There are many edible sections of a wild radish.

The leaves can be collected at any time in their growing cycle, cut into small pieces, and added to salads. They are hot and spicy, so add to other greens. The leaves can also be added to soups, egg dishes, and stews.

The flowers are quite tasty and sweet when you first pick and nibble them, but your mouth will get very hot. Eat them sparingly. You can pick the flowers and add to salads and other dishes as a tasty garnish. The tender flower tips—somewhat resembling Chinese broccoli—can be snapped free, steamed or boiled, and served with butter, cheese, or a spicy sauce.

The green seedpods, which somewhat resemble jalapeño or serrano chiles, can be nibbled when they are still tender inside and haven't gotten woody. You can add the chopped tender pods to soups and salads or try pickling them.

In fact, anything tender on this plant can be eaten, which includes the skin of the root.

RECIPE

Pickled Radish Pods

Pickled radish pods were very popular in the Victorian era. It's a neat way to preserve them, and they're wonderful in salads, sandwiches, or side dishes. It's also very easy to make.

For this recipe, we use ½-pint jars. Simply fill up the jar with as many (clean) radish pods as you can, and in each jar place the following:

2 garlic cloves

½ teaspoon Italian or French spice mix (you can also use dill or other spices of your liking)

1 medium spicy dehydrated chile (just because I like some heat)

⅓ California bay leaf (or ½ regular bay leaf)

½ teaspoon sea salt

In a small saucepan, make a pickling solution composed of 3 parts raw apple cider vinegar and 2 parts white wine. Bring the solution to a boil and pour it into the jars over the radish pods and spices. Close the lids, and place the jars in the fridge. Wait 2–3 weeks before consuming.

If you know how to can and want to preserve them outside the fridge (shelf stable), use the water-bath method, and boil for 15 minutes.

—RECIPE FROM PASCAL BAUDAR

Hedge mustard with sunglasses for size comparison

HEDGE MUSTARD
Sisymbrium irio (aka London rocket) and *S. officinale*

Use: Leaves, raw or cooked
Range: Prefers disturbed soils of fields, roadsides, along trails, farms; can also be found in the desert regions where there is adequate water
Similarity to toxic species: None
Best time: Spring
Status: Common
Tools needed: None

FORAGER NOTE: My brother, Richard, and I took a few trips, typically in winter, through the Southwest (California, Texas, New Mexico, and Arizona). We always tried to collect wild foods to supplement our meals. We usually didn't find much, but we always found hedge mustard and ate the spicy leaves with most of our meals.

Properties

Though there are 41 species of *Sisymbrium* worldwide, we have only 6 in California, and all of them are European natives.

If you already know the mustards (*Brassica* spp.), you will very likely think "mustard" when you see hedge mustard. The flowers of *Sisymbrium* tend to be smaller than the *Brassica* flowers, and the leaflets of the leaves tend to be more "pointy," versus the rounder leaves of *Brassica*. Of course, to botanists, the distinction is mostly in the details of the flowers, but with sufficient observation, you'll be able to recognize hedge mustards by leaf alone.

Hedge mustard leaf, flower, and seed capsules

Uses

I think of *Sisymbrium* as the wild wasabis. Chew on a bit of the leaf and you'll get that hot horseradish-like effect that opens your nostrils. I have friends who turn these leaves into a wild wasabi, which is great on sandwiches, crackers, and as a dip. However, generally I regard hedge mustards as a source of

---

RECIPE

Screaming at the Moon

A hedge mustard soup recipe

2 cups chopped hedge mustard leaves

2 garlic cloves, peeled and crushed

3 cups water

¼ cup miso powder

Simmer the leaves and garlic with the water in a covered pot. When tender, add the miso and cook for another 5 minutes. Makes 2–3 servings.

very spicy greens that go well with salads, soups, egg dishes, sandwiches, stir-fries—just about any dish where you can add greens. These are spicy greens, usually a bit spicier than the greens of common mustards (*Brassicas*).

I have had broths made from the finely diced hedge mustard leaves, into which a lot of rice had been added. This dish was hot and good! I have had "wild kimchee" consisting of wild greens that had been marinating in raw apple cider vinegar. A lot of the hedge mustard leaves were used in one of these kimchees, and it was delicious.

You could also dry the hedge mustard leaves and either reconstitute them later or just powder them and use it as a seasoning.

The flowers are good, too, but they aren't quite as good as the

Two leaves of *S. irio*

Brassica mustard flowers. Hedge mustard flowers seem to have too much of that bitter and astringent bite, so I use them sparingly in soups and salads, but mostly in cooked dishes.

Obviously, this hose hasn't been used much! *Sisymbrium* grows through it.

CACTUS FAMILY (CACTACEAE)

There are 125 genera in the Cactus family and about 1,800 species worldwide, mostly in American deserts. Eleven genera are found in California.

According to Dr. Leonid Enari, the entire Cactus family is a very safe family for consumption. However, he would quickly add that some are much too woody for food. A very few are extremely bitter—even after boiling—and you'd not even consider using them for food.

If you choose to experiment, just remember that palatability is the key. Don't eat any that are too woody or any that are extremely bitter. Any that have a white sap when cut are not cacti but are in fact look-alike members of the *Euphorbia* genus.

Prickly pear pad with cochineal beetle covering it

PRICKLY PEAR
Opuntia spp.

Use: Young pads for food, raw or cooked; fruits for desserts and juices; seeds for flour
Range: Typically found in the desert regions but also commonly found in chaparral, dry fields, along the coast, and commonly cultivated
Similarity to toxic species: Occasionally, people have experienced sickness after eating certain varieties. In some cases, this is due to a negative reaction to the mucilaginous quality; there may be other chemical reasons as well. Therefore, despite this being a very commonly used food for millennia, we suggest you start with very little and monitor your reactions.

Best time: Spring is the best time to collect the new pads, though the older ones can also be used. September through October is the best time for harvesting the fruits.
Status: Common
Tools needed: Metal tongs, sturdy bucket, possibly gloves

Properties

There are 12 species of *Opuntia* in California, not counting varieties; all but 2 are native. We are mostly concerned with the prickly pears—the oval-shaped, flat-padded cacti—because these are the easiest to harvest, prepare, and eat.

The prickly pear cacti are by no means the only variety of cactus commonly observed in California, but they are probably one of the most common cacti in, and on the fringes of, the urban areas. The prickly pear cacti are readily recognized by their flat oval pads, called nopales, with their spines evenly spaced over their surface. The cacti flower by summer and the fruits mature by August and September in a variety of colors, ranging from green (less common) to yellow, orange, red, and purple. Each of these fruits has a different flavor and was traditionally used in different recipes.

Nearly all species of *Opuntia* have a long history of being used for food. The key to using this plant is to find a way to harvest and clean it without getting the spines—and the finer glochids at the base of each spine—in your fingers. The pads are generally easier to harvest, though I still recommend using metal tongs. The very young, still-glossy green pads can be scraped with a sharp knife to remove the spines and glochids and then rinsed before using in a recipe. There is a variety with recessed glochids that I simply leave alone. The fruits tend to have more spines, and I collect them with metal tongs. Still using the tongs, I turn each fruit over in a flame—for about 10 seconds—to burn off the spines and glochids. Then I cut them in half, remove the fruit inside, and eat, preserve, or process it in some way.

Uses

There are several ways to get a meal from the prickly pear cactus: young pad, old pad, fruit, or seed.

FORAGER NOTE: If you collect cacti, you will—sooner or later—get spines and glochids in your skin. Spines are easy to see and relatively easy to remove, but glochids are smaller, hairlike, and more difficult to remove from the skin. Try smearing white glue on the part of your hand that has glochids. Let the glue dry and then peel it off. This technique will usually remove most glochids.

Young prickly pear pad

Whether you pick your pads from the wild or grow cactus in your backyard, the new growth of spring offers one of the more readily available foods with the least amount of work. Remember, nearly all cacti have some spines and tiny little glochids, so you'll need to be careful whether you have very young or very old pads. Moreover, some varieties are less spiny than others; these are the ones I choose. There are also some "spineless" cacti that are easier to handle and clean, though they do contain the small glochids that must be removed.

When you get the very young pads of spring, they are still bright green, and the tough outer layer hasn't yet developed. Carefully pick them, and then you can quickly burn off the young spines or thoroughly scrape each side to remove all spines and glochids. Afterward, you can slice or dice and sauté them to remove much of the liquid and sliminess of the cacti. Cook off the liquid produced by cooking the cacti and then add eggs, potatoes, or even tofu for a delicious stew. Older pads are also edible, but their flavor and texture are different. If you simply cut a large prickly pear pad in half, you'll see that the fiber is all toward the surface. You can carefully slice off the outer fiber layer and use the insides. The flavor and texture resemble squash, and you can use these older cactus pads in soups, stews, or a more traditional manner of cooking with eggs.

Another way to prepare the young pads is to clean, slice, marinate, and dry them. Don't slice these too thin because the pad is mostly water and the dried pieces will be very tiny. Dried cacti "chips" are slightly sour, and you can give them flavor based on the marinade you choose (sweet, sour, salty, etc.; I prefer Bragg's Liquid Aminos, which is an all-purpose seasoning). They make a great snack, can be added to other foods, and will give you the health benefits similar to eating the pads fresh.

Fruits are delicious, too, and are the closest thing, aside from the abundance of tiny seeds, to watermelon that you'll find in the

A ripe cactus fruit

wild. Prickly pear fruits may ripen green, yellow, orange, purple, or red—there are many varieties with subtle flavor differences. I like the yellow the best, but I will harvest whatever I can get. If I am out for a walk and see a few ripe fruits, I will carefully pick them, scrape off the stickers with my pocketknife, slice the fruit in half, and lift out the inner edible portion. However, if there is a large patch that I can harvest, I go with a plastic tub and metal salad tongs. Carefully, I fill the tub with the ripe fruit. Then, at home, using the metal tongs, I quickly pass each fruit through a flame to burn off the glochids and spines before I rinse and wash them. I cut open each fruit and either eat each as is, or I deseed them and store them to use later in such foods as drinks, jams, pie filling, and so on. An excellent drink is made by mixing 50 percent of this cactus fruit puree with 50 percent springwater.

In the old days, even the seeds from the prickly pear fruits were saved, dried, and ground into flour. I've tried it a few times. The flour has a unique flavor, but it's a lot of work.

Medicinal Properties

Eating the prickly pear pads (raw, cooked, or in juice) has long been considered one way to combat diabetes. For those who don't want to grow, clean, and cook their own nopales, you can now purchase the powder that you consume in various ways to combat diabetes. However, there are so many simple and tasty ways to cook and prepare the prickly pear cactus pads that I can't see why anyone would buy the powdered cactus in a pill bottle! But consider this: If you have diabetes and you change your habits and diet to try to cure yourself, but there is no change in your diabetic condition, the worst that can happen is that you have been eating cactus. Thousands of people have died from some of the very drugs that have been introduced in recent decades that were intended to cure diabetes! Sometimes, it's really worthwhile to look to the past for a more fulfilling future.

AMINO ACID PROFILES –
milligrams per gram of dehydrated nopal (cactus pad)

ESSENTIAL AMINO ACIDS	
Histidine	0.08
Isoleucine	2.53
Leucine	5.14
Lysine	4.50
Methionine	0.80
Phenylalanine	2.88
Threonine	1.38
Valine	4.31
NONESSENTIAL AMINO ACIDS	
Alanine	3.95
Arginine	1.26
Aspartic acid	0.32
Cysteine	0.16
Glutamic acid	1.66
Glycine	4.50
Proline	3.48
Serine	0.36
Tyrosine	2.05

From *Prickly Pear Cactus Medicine* by Ran Knishinsky

Cautions
Read "Similarity to toxic species" in the description.

Periodically, I have read and heard that some prickly pears are poisonous (or toxic). It's true that some people react adversely to the mucilaginous quality of the cactus pads, and that seems to be more of an individual aversion. The only exception was a report given to me by Cody Lundin, who described how several people became sick from eating from a certain prickly pear patch in Arizona. We were unable to determine if there was something unique about that

Cactus pads, cleaned and sliced. In the foreground are sliced pads on the food drier tray.

particular cactus patch—perhaps it had something to do with the soil—that caused the sickness.

Considering that all these species of prickly pear have been eaten widely around the world, usually with no regard to species, we can regard prickly pears as a safe and good food. In a review of the ethnobotanical properties of at least 28 species of *Opuntia* in California and beyond, we were unable to find any data about toxic qualities in any of them. Still, anytime you collect foods from the wild, there are factors that are not under your control, so you need to always exercise caution and common sense when collecting and using wild foods.

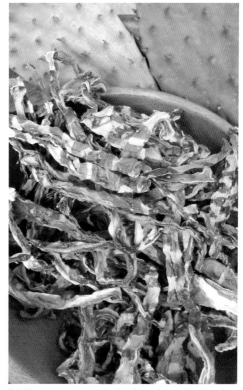

Prickly pear cactus pads that have been sliced and dried

PINK FAMILY (CARYOPHYLLACEAE)

The Pink family consists of 83 to 89 genera (depending on which authority) and about 3,000 species worldwide. Twenty-nine genera are found in California.

Young chickweed in flower

CHICKWEED
Stellaria media

Use: The leaves are best raw in salads but can also be cooked in various dishes or dried and powdered to make into pasta.

Range: Scattered widely where the conditions are ideal: moist and shady areas in the urban setting, mountain canyons, and along rivers

Similarity to toxic species: Also growing with chickweed is scarlet pimpernel, which looks very similar to chickweed except that it has orange flowers and lacks the line of hairs on the stem. You may also find young common spurge (*Euphorbia peplus*) in chickweed patches, which superficially resembles the chickweed, but spurge doesn't have the line of white hairs, its stalk is more erect, and the leaves are alternate, not opposite like chickweed. Break the stem of spurge and you will see a white sap; it shouldn't be eaten.

Best time: Spring; chickweed rarely lasts beyond midsummer.
Status: Common
Tools needed: None

Properties

There are 190 species of *Stellaria* worldwide, with 13 of those found in California, 9 of which are native; the other 4 are introduced from Europe. Common chickweed is one of the 4 introduced species of *Stellaria* that is now very common in California. In fact, it now can be found worldwide.

Chickweed is common in urban yards, in shady fields, and in mountain canyons. It is a short-lived annual that shrivels up by summer when the soil is dry.

Young chickweed. Note flower buds.

Chickweed is a low-growing, sprawling annual that first arises after the winter rains. The thin stem will grow up to 1' long, and upon close inspection, you'll see a line of fine white hairs along one side of the stem. The oval-shaped leaves, arranged in pairs along the stem, come to a sharp tip. The flowers are white and 5-petaled, though they may appear to have 10 petals because each petal has a deep cleft.

Here's a quick comparison of chickweed and common spurge.

	CHICKWEED	COMMON SPURGE
LEAF ARRANGEMENT	Opposite	Alternate
LEAF TIP	Pointed	Round
STEM	Weak, sprawling; green	Erect; green to red
HAIRS	Single line on stem	None
SAP	None	White sap visible when stem is broken
FLOWER	White, 5 petals, each with deep cleft	Yellowish green; inconspicuous

Uses

Chickweed is probably best used as a salad plant. In a thick patch of chickweed, one can cut off a handful of the stems just above the root. Then you rinse the leaves, dice, and add salad dressing.

RECIPE

Mia's Chickweed Soup

Although chickweed is found in common city sidewalks, it's best to gather it in the wild, away from pesticides. As homage to its humble origins, I call this my "sidewalk soup." It's simple and low-fat (you can omit the pancetta or bacon, and it's still amazing) and has a surprising depth of flavor reminiscent of spring peas and pea shoots. This is my version of "wild split pea soup."

4–5 tablespoons diced pancetta (or you can use bacon)

1 medium onion, diced

1 stalk celery

1 carrot

1 teaspoon olive oil, or as needed

4–5 cloves garlic, finely minced

1 teaspoon fennel seeds

1 small California bay leaf

1 small California white sage leaf

2 teaspoons French or Italian herbs (I like oregano, thyme, parsley)

1 small potato, cubed

6 cups packed washed and chopped chickweed

1 teaspoon raw apple cider vinegar (to keep mixture green)

Olive oil, salt, and pepper to taste

In a heated stockpot, sauté the pancetta or bacon until crisp and then add onion, celery, and carrot and sauté until translucent. You may need to add a bit of olive oil to the bottom of the pan; start with 1 teaspoon. Add the garlic and spices and continue to sauté until just fragrant. Add the cubed potato; it will serve to thicken the soup once pureed. Add the chickweed (save a handful for garnish), and add enough water to cover the chickweed with an inch of water. Cover and bring to a boil. Add the vinegar and then reduce to a light simmer for about 20–30 minutes.

Once slightly cooled, transfer to a food processor and puree the mixture. Serve with tender, crisp chickweed as garnish. Delish!

—RECIPE FROM MIA WASILEVICH

Young chickweed

The plant can also be cooked in soups and stews. For those who are more adventurous, the entire aboveground chickweed plant can be dried, powdered, mixed 50-50 with wheat flour, and run through a pasta machine. The result is a green pasta with the flavor of chickweed.

A mash of fresh chickweed leaves will help to allay the pain and swelling from mosquito bites. I've personally found this more efficacious than the more widely suggested plantain leaf. We've also found that at least one Amish family sells dried and powdered chickweed in a salve to be used for mosquito bites.

Because chickweed grows close to the ground with its fine stems, it is common to find other plants growing in chickweed patches. You need to make certain you are only collecting chickweed. We've seen poison hemlock growing within chickweed patches.

Fresh chickweed collected, rinsed, and ready for salad

GOOSEFOOT FAMILY (CHENOPODIACEAE)

The Goosefoot family consists of 100 genera and about 1,500 species. It is found worldwide, especially in the deserts, as well as in saline or alkaline soils. Some species are cultivated for food. There are 19 genera in California. According to Dr. Leonid Enari, this is one of those very promising plant families for food. His research indicated that most of the leaves could be used for food, either raw or cooked if too bitter and unpalatable. Dr. Enari also stated that the majority of the seeds could be harvested, winnowed, ground, and used for a flour or flour extender.

Orach plant RICK ADAMS

ORACH
Atriplex californica

Use: Leaves can be used raw, if palatable, or cooked; dried for seasoning.
Range: Restricted to California beaches; can be cultivated
Similarity to toxic species: None
Best time: Spring
Status: Somewhat common
Tools needed: None

Young orach plant on the beach RICK ADAMS

Properties

The *Atriplex* genus has about 250 species worldwide, all generally known as salt-bush or orach. There are 43 species of *Atriplex* in California, not including varie-ties. Most are native.

When most folks see orach for the first time, they think it is a lamb's quar-ter plant with pointy leaves. Orach does resemble lamb's quarter, except that it is pretty much restricted to the coastal regions. Look closely at each leaf. The color is very much like lamb's quarter, except that the leaf has 2 bottom barbs that make it look similar to an arrowhead. Also, look closely at the young leaves, and you will note that the very edge of the leaf has the red tint that you often see in the stems of lamb's quarter.

The plant is found along the beaches and in the back bays. It grows about 2' tall and has inconspicuous flowers.

Orach is easy to grow in your backyard garden. Once it's planted and goes to seed, it will reseed itself indefinitely, as long as the conditions are suitable.

Uses

Orach is used more or less as you'd use lamb's quarter, except it's a bit saltier and sometimes more bitter. This means that sometimes you wouldn't use orach in salads, unless very sparingly for that salty flavor. On the other hand, I have eaten raw orach leaves that were mild and tasty and wonderful in salads. The soil, time of year, and age of the plant all seem to play a role in the palatability of orach.

Orach leaf RICK ADAMS

The young orach leaves can also be boiled like spinach and eaten alone. Changing the water and cooking again usually improves the flavor. More people will probably enjoy the leaves when added to mixed greens, vegetable stew, or soup, or added sparingly to rice or egg dishes.

Try drying and powdering the orach leaves and then using as a salt substitute. Try it sparingly at first, because it could be very strong.

Green lamb's quarter, *C. murale*

LAMB'S QUARTER, WHITE AND GREEN
Chenopodium album and *C. murale*

Use: Leaves used raw or cooked; seeds added to soups or bread batter; leaves dried for seasoning
Range: Prefers disturbed soils of farms, gardens, hillsides, fields, along trails, etc.
Similarity to toxic species: Western black nightshade leaves can be confused with lamb's quarter leaves when very young. Be sure to look for the white mealy (and "sparkly") underside of lamb's quarter and for the streak of red in the axils.
Best time: Spring for the leaves; late summer for the seeds
Status: Common and widespread
Tools needed: None

Properties
Chenopodium has about 100 species worldwide, and 24 are in California, not including varieties; 17 are native.

Lamb's quarter is a plant that everyone has seen but probably not recognized. It's an annual plant that sprouts up in the spring and summer in fields, gardens, and disturbed soils, and generally it grows about 3'–4' tall. (I did record one *C. album* at 12', but that's the exception.) I've even seen it growing in the cracks in the sidewalks and alleys of downtown Los Angeles.

The leaf shape is roughly triangular, somewhat resembling a goose or duck's foot, hence the family name. The color of the stem and leaves is light green, and the axils of the leaves (and sometimes the stem) are streaked with red. The bottom of each leaf is covered with a mealy substance, causing raindrops to bead up on the leaf.

As the plant matures in the season, inconspicuous green flowers will appear, and seeds will form as the plant dries and withers.

Uses

Lamb's quarter is a versatile plant that can be used in many recipes. The young tender leaves can be cut into small pieces and used in

White lamb's quarter, *C. album,* after a rain

a salad. The leaves and tender stems can be cooked like spinach and seasoned for a tasty dish, and the cooking water makes a delicious broth. The leaves can also be added to soups, egg dishes, quiche, and even stir-fries with other vegetables.

In California, lamb's quarter will go to seed by late summer, and seeds from the dead plant are harvestable for several months. The seed is an excellent source of calcium, phosphorus, and potassium, according to the USDA. Collect the seeds by hand, place in a large salad bowl, and then rub them between your hands to remove the chaff. Next, winnow them by letting handfuls drop into the salad bowl as you gently blow off the chaff. The seeds are then added to soup and rice dishes and bread batter. Alternatively, just cook the winnowed lamb's quarter seed and serve with butter and/ or other seasonings. Think of it as "poor man's quinoa." Quinoa (*Chenopodium quinoa*) is a close relative of lamb's quarter.

A view of the small lamb's quarter seed, the wild version of quinoa

White lamb's quarter, *C. album,* growing in cement

Cautions

Older leaves may cause slight irritation to the throat if eaten raw without dressing.

Though the common *Chenopodium* species are fairly easy to recognize, there is one called soaproot (*C. californicum*) whose leaves are very unpalatable, even when cooked, and whose root is a great source of soap. Though you could make wonderful soap by shaving the root and mixing it with water, you'd not want to eat this. Let your taste buds be your guide, as in this case.

The freshly harvested leaf, ready to be processed into soup and salad

Young glasswort growing in sand

GLASSWORT OR PICKLEWEED
Salicornia spp.

Use: Use the tender stems raw, cooked, or pickled.
Range: Found along the Pacific Coast above high tide, along the rivers that feed into the ocean, and in the back-bay areas
Similarity to toxic species: None
Best time: Spring
Status: Common locally
Tools needed: Clippers

Properties
There are 50 species of *Salicornia* worldwide. Five species are found in California, and all are native.

Glasswort is typically found in the back bays and sand flats above the high-tide areas of the Pacific Ocean. I have seen acres of nearly all glasswort in such

Young glasswort in sand

places. However, it will also grow somewhat solitary and in some of the fields and wild areas not too far from beaches.

The plant stems—about ¼" thick—can have the appearance of swollen pencils, but not as thick, with distinct joints. The stalks are a pale green color—almost translucent—and turn red in the fall. The entire plant rises no more than a few inches high. There are no apparent leaves. There are flowers and seeds, but these are usually very inconspicuous. The overall appearance of the plant is of small, swollen stalks.

Uses

Glasswort makes a great beachside nibble—a little here, and a little there. It's also good added to salads, but not too much. Just gently pinch the tender tips and add it sparingly to salads, because in volume, it may be a bit too strong and can overpower your salad. Plus, you need to gather it young enough before it begins to get woody and becomes largely inedible.

Cooked, glasswort's flavor is just right when added to soups, chowder, and even omelets. I suggest you taste a little first and experiment before adding a lot to your dishes. In some cases, you might find that the flavor is greatly improved

Maturing glasswort RICK ADAMS

by boiling the tender stems, pouring off the water, and adding the glasswort to your various cooked dishes.

I have enjoyed very simple pickled glasswort, too. Just collect the tender young sections of the stems before they get woody on the inside. Pack them loosely in a jar, cover with raw apple cider vinegar, and put in your refrigerator. In about a month, they will make a great garnish and side for various dishes.

You could also make your glasswort pickles a bit milder by boiling them briefly, rinsing them of the water, and then putting them into a glass jar with vinegar.

Russian thistle RICK ADAMS

RUSSIAN THISTLE
Salsola tragus (formerly *S. kali*)

Use: Very young new growth can be cooked and eaten.
Range: Though seemingly a stereotypical plant of the desert, Russian thistle is somewhat widespread in valleys, fields, disturbed soils, and the fringes of the urban sprawl.
Similarity to toxic species: None
Best time: Spring
Status: Can be common locally and seasonally
Tools needed: None

FORAGER NOTE: This plant is native to Central Asia and eastern Russia. The United States purchased flaxseed from Russia in 1874, and the Russian thistle seed was in the flax. Russian thistle thus made its first appearance in North America in Scotland, South Dakota.

Properties

There are about 100 species of *Salsola* worldwide. In California, there are 7 species, and all of them are introduced.

Everyone seems to know Russian thistle (aka tumbleweed) from Westerns: large, dry, round plants that blow across the plains via the wind. However, while that is somewhat accurate, there is nothing edible when the plants mature into those large, dry balls.

It is the very young new and tender growth that can be used. The color of the stalk and leaves is pale green, almost a shade of blue, and the leaves are spiny and shaped like needles, maybe 1"–2" in length. These leaves are covered with fine hairs, and you can usually observe some red in the axils and on the stalks.

Russian thistle close-up shows the papery flower and the stems.

Interestingly, though a very inconspicuous plant, it produces an equally inconspicuous flower that is actually very beautiful if you take the time to observe it. The flowers are small and measure approximately ⅛"–¼" across, and they consist of sepals that appear fragile and paperlike; there are no petals. These flowers are formed individually in the upper axils of the plant.

As the plant matures and gets older, it turns into the dry, round ball up to 3' in diameter, and when its small root is broken free by the wind, it rolls over the countryside and spreads as many as 200,000 winged seeds per plant. No wonder it's everywhere!

Uses

Our main source of food here are the young, tender leaves. Collect them individually so you know they are still tender. I usually simply boil and serve with butter. They can also be served plain or with cheese.

Once boiled, taste the juice. It's actually a pretty good broth. You can drink it plain or use it as a soup base.

If I am mixing Russian thistle with other vegetables or greens, I will chop it up a bit first. If the leaves are tender enough, they could be boiled and then mixed into a casserole or even a meat loaf–type dish.

Sometimes, if you get the very young shoots of the Russian thistle, you can quickly dip them into boiling water to reduce their fibrous surfaces. They can then be used in raw dishes without experiencing any irritation to the throat.

A view of the needlelike leaf segments

STONECROP FAMILY (CRASSULACEAE)

This family contains about 33 genera and about 1,400 species worldwide, with 7 genera found in California.

Dudleya grows in the cracks in rocks. RICK ADAMS

LIVE-FOREVER
Dudleya spp.

Use: Leaves as a nibble, in salads, cooked
Range: In the rocks in chaparral and mountain areas
Similarity to toxic species: None
Best time: Spring, but can be used year-round
Status: Not common
Tools needed: None

Properties

The *Dudleya* genus contains about 46 members, and 26 (not counting subspecies) of these are in California, all of which are native. Some are common, but there are some that are not common; at least 3 are rare, and 1 is an endangered species. Do your homework before eating any of these. One is called *D. edulis.* How do you think it got that name? Because it's edible! This little succulent plant is typically found growing right out of the cracks in rock hillsides and cliffs. This seems like a harsh environment, but that's where the *Dudleya* prefers to call home.

The plant's pointed succulent leaves are formed in a rosette. The plants have the appearance of a rose flower, if you can imagine each petal being a succulent pale blue leaf. The flower stalk arises a few inches. Each flower has 5 petals, typically pale orange to red.

Uses

Though I'd nibbled on the succulent and sometimes astringent leaves of *Dudleya* many times, the first time I'd taken the plant seriously was when a friend took me on a "short hike" to do some exploring. I didn't bring along water because I was told it would be "only a mile." Well, the hike was more than a mile, and it was entirely downhill with at least 1,000' elevation decline over rocky boulders. I knew I would not be going back the way I came. I took the long way back to my car, about 8 miles. There was no water; there was no cactus. I found and began to pick the *Dudleya* leaves. I chewed one, and it was fleshy and succulent, not astringent. I kept many in my pocket. Though they did not quench my thirst, they did give my body needed moisture, and I got back feeling OK and without dehydration.

The leaves and the tender flowering stems were eaten by the Cahuilla of Southern California in the springtime and were regarded as a delicacy.

I've occasionally added a few of the leaves to salad. The palatability of these leaves depends on the soil and the amount of rainfall during the previous winter. Sometimes, the leaves are a bit too astringent to eat raw in salads, and they are improved when cooking. Once cooked, the leaves are usually very mild, even bland, and will take on the flavor of whatever spices you use.

Dudleya

HEATH FAMILY (ERICACEAE)

The Heath family contains about 100 genera and more than 3,000 species world-wide. In California, there are 26 genera of this family, and *Arctostaphylos* is the largest genus.

The manzanita tree RICK ADAMS

MANZANITA
Arctostaphylos spp.

Use: Berries for beverage, food additive; leaves for medicine
Range: Different species found in the mountains, chaparral, and even the desert
Similarity to toxic species: None
Best time: About September for berries
Status: Relatively widespread
Tools needed: None

Properties

In California, there are at least 62 species (not counting subspecies) of *Arctostaphylos* that we refer to as some sort of manzanita. All are native. They typically have characteristic dark red or maroon-colored bark, often with a shredded look. They have the appearance of small trees or bushes. At least one is vining.

The leaves are alternate, evergreen, generally round- to ovate-shaped, a bit leathery, and stiff. The flowers are similar to little white lanterns or urns that hang from the plant, and the flower parts are usually in 5s. The flowers mature

Immature manzanita berry. Note the leaf shape. RICK ADAMS

into round, reddish fruits; they actually vary slightly in color from an orange-yellow to a darker maroon color. Some have a very sticky surface, and some are very dry on the surface.

They can be found in a broad array of environments: rocky slopes, upper chaparral, throughout parts of the desert, in woodlands, and so on.

Uses

Though the manzanita berries are only available seasonally, generally peaking around September, sometimes they are found in abundance and can also be dried for later use.

There are some species whose berries are sticky on the surface and others that are not. I prefer those that are not sticky, because less dirt sticks to them and less cleaning is needed.

There are several ways to enjoy the manzanita berries. The ripened berries can simply be brewed in warm water to make a pleasant lemonade-like drink. While there's sugar content, it's also sour, and you can enjoy this drink hot or cold—while sitting around the campfire or with a few fruits in your canteen for a trail drink.

Traditionally, the mature and dried berries would be gently ground on a rock or in something like a *molcajete* (traditional Mexican stone grinding bowl). The flour, strained from the seeds, can then be used in many ways: added to other bread products (like acorn flour) as an emulsifier or smoothener, added to various batters, or just added to water for a drink.

The seeds can be boiled for a strong vinegar-flavored liquid. You can use this as substitute vinegar for your salad dressings or dilute it with water and sweeten it for a good wild lemonade.

Kinnikinnick was an old-time smoking mix made from one of the desert manzanitas. I've used many of the leaves this way, just drying and then crumbling them fine. They smoke well, have a decent aroma, and there's no harmful side effect as with tobacco.

Another old-time native use from Northern California is to make an infusion from the leaves and drink it to cure poison oak rash. Though I have never had to try this, I have heard some firsthand reports that this works quickly and effectively.

Mature manzanita berries

LEGUME FAMILY (FABACEAE)

This is a big family worldwide, with about 730 genera and 19,400 species. In California, this large group is represented by 50 genera.

Acacia pods RICK ADAMS

ACACIA
Acacia spp.

Use: Seeds for food; leaves for medicinal tea
Range: Planted commonly in the urban areas; escaped in local fields, parks, chaparral
Similarity to toxic species: Because there are several toxic members of the Pea family, be sure you've properly identified acacia pods and seeds.
Best time: Seeds mature in early summer.
Status: Common locally
Tools needed: None

Properties

The *Acacia* genus includes about 960 species worldwide, with 7 species in California. These are generally called acacia or wattle, and most are originally from Australia. The native catclaw plant had formerly been classified an *Acacia*, but it has been recently reclassified by botanists as *Senegalia greggii*.

Hanging acacia pods

Various acacia shrubs and trees are typically planted as park, street, and yard trees, and many have gone wild.

The tree's leaves are bipinnately divided, giving the tree an overall ferny look. The bright yellow flowers appear to form balls or globes and make the tree very conspicuous when in flower. In the summer, the flat pods can be seen hanging from the trees. Small black seeds fall to the ground as the pods mature.

Uses

Not widely known is that the seeds from the pods were once good food back home in Australia. The Aboriginal people considered the larger seeds, which they called mulga, a great source of food. Mulga seeds are at least as large as a green pea, maybe a bit larger. The mature seeds would be dried and ground into flour that could be used in a variety of ways; one traditional way was to add water and form a large pancake, which was cooked right on the coals of a campfire. Such a pancake is known as damper, and mulga damper was a regular staple back in old Australia.

Unfortunately, we don't have the larger mulga seeds in California. Among others, we have the black wattle acacia, also sometimes called silver wattle (*A.*

Acacia bowl

dealbata), which is somewhat common as a gone-wild park tree in parts of California. We have collected these smaller seeds off the ground and by picking the mature pods from the tree. Once a sufficient volume of the seeds was collected, we ground them in a *molcajete* until we had flour. We blended the flour with additional wheat flour and acorn flour, added water, and formed biscuits. We cooked these by the fire until done, and everyone found them quite delicious.

The leaves are used as a somewhat flavorless tea when a mild astringent is needed—for example, for a sore throat—or the tea can be used as an external wash for sunburns, insect bites, scrapes, abrasions, and other skin irritations.

Acacia seed

Mature carob pods in a *molcajete*

CAROB
Ceratonia siliqua

Use: Ripened pods for food, excluding the seed
Range: Mostly an urban street tree
Similarity to toxic species: None
Best time: Pods ripen in late summer into fall
Status: Somewhat common
Tools needed: Bags

Properties
Carob is from the Middle East, but tens of thousands have been planted in Southern California as a street and park tree. They get large, nearly as large as a coast live oak, with a large trunk as it matures.

This is an evergreen tree with pinnately divided leaves, each leaflet more or less round. In the flowering stage, the tree is very aromatic, and sometimes (once you know the smell), you can detect carob trees while driving down a street.

The pods begin in the spring as thick green pods, approximately 6"–8" long (there are plenty of smaller and larger ones). When the pods mature in summer, they are brown and leathery. Mature pods drop from the trees slowly, so some will be on the tree much of the year.

Uses

Mature carob pods are delicious just picked off the tree or ground and eaten. When you pick a fruit, break it open and make sure it is entirely ripe with no green inside. The ones that aren't entirely ripe will be a bit astringent. Clean them and discard any that have been eaten by animals or are already very wormy inside.

Carob leaf

The ripe carob pod is probably the closest thing to the ultimate survival food that you're likely ever to find. Rich in natural sugar, palatable, high in the B vitamins for protein, rich in calcium—it is good for you, and it tastes delicious too!

The pods can be eaten raw with no particular preparation besides cleaning, and they will last for years, so you can just fill your pack with carob pods and eat them when you're hungry.

However, what if you want some carob milk shakes or carob candy? Well, then you should just go to the store and buy some! It's quite an ordeal to make a carob milk shake with the pods unless you have a way to grind the pods into a very fine meal. Most home processors just won't do it. First, you need to crack open the pods and remove the very hard seeds. Then you grind the pods, usually several times, until you get the finest meal. The best I was ever able to do at home was to get brownish milk with all the carob meal settling to the bottom of the glass without dissolving. As for carob candy, most that you buy is just another junk food to which a bit of carob has been added. However, you can remove and discard the seeds, grind the pods into a flour, and add that sweet flour to cake, bread, cookies, muffins, and even pie fillings. I have seen whole cookbooks describing how to process the mature carob pod into dozens of products.

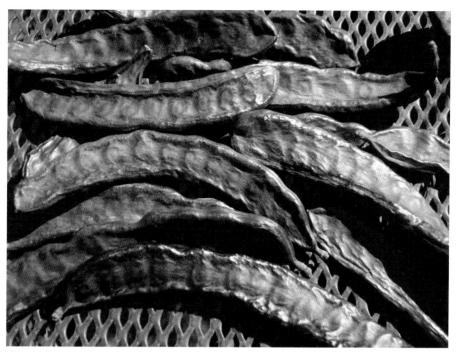
Ripe carob pods

But at the end of the day, I just like to eat the pods as they are, with the seeds removed. They are tasty, nutritious, and make a very easy snack.

Caution
Be sure to bite into the pod carefully and to spit out the very hard seeds.

Palo verde tree

PALO VERDE
Parkinsonia microphylla and *P. florida*

Use: Seeds are eaten green or dried and ground into flour
Range: Southeastern part of the state; sometimes cultivated
Similarity to toxic species: Some pods or pealike capsules from this family can be toxic. Always make sure you have accurately identified any member of this family that you intend to eat.
Best time: Green pods in early summer; mature pods in late summer to fall
Status: Scattered within its range
Tools needed: None

Properties
There are 11 or 12 species of *Parkinsonia* worldwide. Three species are found in California, and the 2 listed above are native.

Palo verde tree leaf and flower

This plant ranges from a large shrub to a smallish tree; it is deciduous, with bark that is somewhat green, which is where the name comes from. The alternately arranged, bipinnately divided leaves are long and graceful, giving the plant a very feathery appearance. There are thorns in the leaf axils. The conspicuous flowers are divided into 5 yellow petals with 10 distinct stamens. It's a good bee attractor. The multiseeded pods hang from the trees. One easy way to tell the difference between these 2 species is that the pod of *P. florida* (blue palo verde) is of an even thickness and sometimes slightly narrowed between the seeds; however, the pods of *P. microphylla* (yellow palo verde) are distinctly narrow between the seeds. The tree is not particularly common but is used more and more for landscaping, as it is drought tolerant and beautiful when it flowers. In the wild, it's found in the southeastern deserts of California, into Arizona, and down into Baja.

FORAGER NOTE: Because these trees are both beautiful and drought tolerant, we are seeing more of them in the urban and suburban areas in drought-tolerant landscapes. This provides an opportunity for the urban forager.

Uses

The seeds are the prize of this tree. The Cahuilla and Yuma people (among others) ate the whole pod while it was still green. Once the seedpods were dry and mature, the seeds were removed and the thin shell discarded. The very hard seeds were then typically ground into a flour and used as a meal. Generally, the flour from palo verde would be made into porridge or something similar to cakes or biscuits. The whole seeds have also been simply parched almost until being burned and then eaten. Some of the tribes sprouted the seeds before eating them.

The little seeds are hard when they mature, and you don't just chew on a dry, hard seed. They need to be ground on a rock or

Palo verde pods and seeds in a *molcajete,* ready to turn into flour

molcajete into a flour. This contrasts with mesquite, where the entire pod and seed are used, and carob, where the seeds are discarded and the pod is eaten.

Interestingly, this is often referred to as a survival food. When I hear the term "survival food," I think of something that you'd never eat unless you were desperate and starving—things such as bark and lichens. Perhaps it is thought of this way because the plant is not all that common and because other tastier seeds were usually available to some of the desert people.

Bark, leaves, and flowers of the mesquite. Note the thorns. RICK ADAMS

MESQUITE
Prosopis glandulosa and *P. pubescens* (screwbean), both natives

Use: Pods used for food
Range: Lower deserts
Similarity to toxic species: None
Best time: Pods begin to form in spring and mature in summer.
Status: Widespread within its zone
Tools needed: None

Mesquite thorns RICK ADAMS

Traditional Southern California Mesquite Bean Cake

These rich, molasses-like cakes were used as travel food by Indians, with pieces broken off and eaten or reconstituted in water to make a drink that could be hot or cold.

I am not a doctor, but I have read that mesquite digests slowly and helps maintain stable blood sugar, which is important for diabetics. It's also high in protein and fiber. ***Note:*** Everything in these recipes must be taken at your own risk. As always, do your research or consult your physician.

Mix ground, whole-bean dried mesquite flour (I get mine from the Seri Indians) into boiling water, reduce heat, and stir into a thick mush (or *atole*). Simmer and stir a few minutes longer to tenderize (especially if the flour is coarsely ground) and then blend in additional flour until the mixture thickens and stiffens enough to hold shape. Form into cakes 2"–4" in diameter and about ½" thick on a cookie sheet or tinfoil and dry in the sun or on rocks near a fire. As an alternative, I generally place them in a preheated oven at 300°F for 2 hours, until the cakes have dried a bit, and then I reduce the heat to 150°F or less for 3–4 hours. Once removed from the oven, I leave them out for even more time to dry more thoroughly. One cup flour makes a large cake for about 4.

—RECIPE FROM PAUL CAMPBELL, AUTHOR OF *SURVIVAL SKILLS OF NATIVE CALIFORNIA*

Properties

There are 44 species of *Prosopis* worldwide, with 3 found in California.

Mesquite is very common throughout the low desert; screwbean, a close relative, is not so common. You've driven past mesquite if you've traveled around Palm Springs. If the plant isn't in flower or fruit, it's somewhat inconspicuous, and you may not have known it was mesquite. The leaf is even pinnately divided into smaller round or linear segments, giving the plant a ferny look. There are little spines on the stems, generally 2 per node.

The mesquite fruits that appear in the summer are pale yellow, dry, and maybe 6" long. They look like slightly withered green beans, except they are yellow when mature.

When not in flower or fruit, mesquite and screwbean are very hard to discern. However, when in fruit, the screwbean is just as the name implies: a bean that looks as if you twisted it. It's somewhat shorter than the mesquite fruit and round in the cross section. It's one big spiral screwed-up bean! (No offense intended.)

Mesquite pods RICK ADAMS

Uses

The yellow pods of mesquite are the main prize of this desert shrub or tree. They are harvested when ripe, which is typically sometime in the summer. There are a number of ways in which the pods have been used for food over the centuries. Perhaps one of the simplest is just to pick the mature pod, chew it, and spit out the seeds. (The screwbean is used similarly.)

Traditionally, the whole pods would be ground into a flour that could be used alone or mixed with other flours to make breads and cakes.

OAK FAMILY (FAGACEAE)

The Oak family includes 7 genera and about 900 species worldwide. There are 3 genera in California, and *Quercus* is the most widespread. There are 25 species of *Quercus* in California, not including subspecies. California's only common non-native is holly oak (*Q. ilex*), which comes from the Mediterranean. Once processed, the nuts of all varieties of acorns can be eaten.

Also included here is tanbark oak, or tan oak (*Notholithocarpus densiflorus*). This tree was once called *Quercus densiflora,* but it has been reclassified into a different genus because of a few key differences. To the average person looking at this tree, it's very much an oak whose acorn caps appear "shaggy." Otherwise, it is used just like any other acorn. *Notholithocarpus* is one of the 3 genera of the Oak family in California, and the tanbark oak is the only species (with 2 varieties) of this genus. (The third genus of this family found in California is the chinquapin.)

A bowl of collected acorns

OAK TREE
Quercus spp.

Use: Acorns used for food once leached; miscellaneous craft and dye uses
Range: Some oaks can be found in nearly every environment of California.
Similarity to toxic species: The tannic acid in acorns is considered toxic, but it's so bitter that you'd never eat enough to get sick or cause a problem.

Best time: Acorns mature from mid-September to as late as early February.

Status: Common

Tools needed: A bag

Properties

Some oak trees are deciduous, and some are evergreen, and the leaf shapes vary from simple to pinnately lobed. Some are bushes, but most are massive. To know your local oaks, you should go to an arboretum or take a plant society walk. Oak trees are very common. They are ubiquitous, and they epitomize the native landscape of California.

The fruit of all oak trees is the acorn, which every child can recognize. Some acorns are fat, some are long and thin, and the caps can vary significantly. Still, the nut set in a scaly cap is universally recognized as the acorn. You should have no trouble recognizing acorns wherever you live.

Uses

The nut from the oak tree is the acorn, and the acorn is a wonderful source of a starchy food. Though I have three separate cookbooks devoted entirely to using acorns in the modern kitchen, I generally only use acorns for cookies, pancakes, and bread.

In the old days, acorns were an important source of food for Native Americans. Acorns were typically collected, dried, and then stored. For use, the acorns were shelled; guess what—they're a bit easier to shell when dried. They were ground and then placed on a sloping rock

Coast live oak acorns RICK ADAMS

with a lip at the lower end or some other variation of a colander. Cold or hot water poured over the acorn meal would wash out the tannic acid. The meal was most often used as a thickener in soups and stews, making a type of gravy.

Acorns were such an important food that every tribe had their own way of processing them, and therefore there was a lot of variety in how this would have been done. There was a lot of lore surrounding the types of acorns; the acorn meal sometimes had a religious significance and would have been used in various ceremonies, in much the way that corn or corn pollen is often used.

The availability of acorns to California tribes was as important in their social development as was agriculture to other cultures. Acorns were a more or less guaranteed food source, and thus they provided a stable foundation upon which the other aspects of the

Angelo Cervera grinds shelled acorns on the metate.

society could grow. Moreover, you didn't just go collect acorns wherever you wanted. Families controlled the various oak groves, and thus they controlled the access to the acorns, which represented political power.

Today, on the trail or in the kitchen, the neatest and quickest way to process the acorns is first to shell them, then boil them and change the water repeatedly until they are no longer bitter. At that point, after drying, I prefer to process

RECIPE

Tongva Memories

Use processed acorn flour (with tannic acid removed), mixed 50-50 with wheat flour and an appropriate amount of water. The dough is then formed into small loaves and cooked on a soapstone slab.

them through a hand-crank meat grinder to produce a coarse meal. Ground finer, which you can do in a coffee grinder, the meal is perfect for any product calling for flour. I typically mix the acorn flour 50-50 with wheat or other flours. This is partly for flavor and partly because acorn flour doesn't hold together as well as wheat flour, for example.

The more traditional method of processing first involves shelling the acorns and then grinding them while still raw. I typically do this on a large, flat-rock metate. Then the meal is put into some sort of primitive colander and water (hot or cold) is poured through it. There were many possible ways to create a colander in the old days; today I just put a cotton cloth inside a large colander and pour cold water over the acorns. Cold water helps to retain the oil and, therefore, the flavor of the acorn meal. The water takes a while to trickle out, and it may require pouring up to 3 or 4 gallons of water through the meal before it is no longer bitter and can be eaten.

I have had modern acorn products of chips, pound cake, and pasta. They are delicious. If I had to describe the acorn flavor, I would say that products made with acorn flour have a subtle graham cracker flavor.

How good are acorns for you? Here are some details from a chart that was published in *Temalpakh: Cahuilla Indian Knowledge and Usage of Plants* by Lowell John Bean and Katherine S. Saubel. Their source was Martin A. Baumhoff, *Ecological Determinants of Aboriginal California Populations* (Berkeley: University of California Press, 1936, p. 162) as modified by Carl Brandt Wolf, *California Wild Tree Crops* (Claremont, CA: Rancho Santa Ana Botanic Garden, 1945, table 1) and William S. Spencer, *Handbook of Biological Data* (New York: W. B. Saunders Co., 1956, table 156).

Chemical Composition of Hulled Acorns (in percent)

Species	Water	Protein	Fats	Fiber	Carbohydrates	Ash	Total proteins, fats, carbohydrates
Q. lobata	9.0	4.9	5.5	9.5	69.0	2.1	79
Q. garryana	9.0	3.9	4.5	12.0	68.9	1.8	77
Q. douglasii	9.0	5.5	8.1	9.8	65.5	2.1	79
Q. chrysolepis	9.0	4.1	8.7	12.7	63.5	2.0	76
Q. agrifolia	9.0	6.3	16.8	11.6	54.6	1.8	78
Q. kelloggii	9.0	4.6	18.0	11.4	55.5	1.6	78
Barley	10.1	8.7	1.9	5.7	71.0	2.6	82
Wheat	12.5	12.3	1.8	2.3	69.4	1.7	84

GERANIUM FAMILY (GERANIACEAE)

Worldwide, there are 6 genera and about 750 species in this family. In California, this family is represented by *California* (1 species), *Erodium, Geranium,* and *Pelargonium.* The latter 2 are widely planted as garden ornamentals and are mostly introduced.

Filaree leaf RICK ADAMS

FILAREE
Erodium spp.

Use: The leaves are used, raw, cooked, or juiced.

Range: Filaree prefers lawns, fields, cultivated and disturbed soils, and the fringes of the urban wilderness.

Similarity to toxic species: Because filaree superficially resembles a fern, and perhaps a member of the Parsley or Carrot family (when not in flower), make sure you are thoroughly familiar with filaree before eating any.

Best time: Spring

Status: Somewhat common

Tools needed: None

Filaree flower RICK ADAMS

Properties

There are 74 species of *Erodium* worldwide. Six of these species can be found in California, and only 1 is a native.

Filaree is a very common urban weed that can be found in gardens, grasslands, and fields, and there are varieties that are found in the desert as well. This annual plant is a low-growing rosette of pinnately compound leaves, which are covered with short hairs. The stalk is fleshy. Sometimes people will think they are looking at a fern when they see filaree. The small, 5-petaled spring flowers are purple, followed by the very characteristic needlelike fruits.

Uses

Filaree with seed capsules

Filaree leaves and stalks can be picked when young and enjoyed in salads. The leaves are a little fibrous but sweet. I pick the entire leaf, including the long stem, for salads or other dishes. They are best chopped up before adding to salads or cooked dishes such as soups or stews.

The plant is quite common and widespread, though the leaves are much smaller when found growing in dry or hard soil.

You might enjoy simply picking the tender stems and chewing on only the stems. They are sweet and tasty, somewhat reminiscent of celery. In fact, sometimes in a dry year I find that the stem part is the only part that I will eat. An older leafy section is drier and more fibrous and lends itself to being added to a stew or other cooked dish.

In wet seasons, the spring growth of filaree is more succulent and tasty. In dry years, the season will be short, and the leaves and stems of filaree will be less desirable.

RECIPE

If you have a wheatgrass juicer, you can process some of the filaree leaves and then enjoy the sweet green juice.

GOOSEBERRY FAMILY (GROSSULARIACEAE)

This family includes only the *Ribes* genus. There are 120 species worldwide, and 31 species are in California, not including varieties. These are found in all environments.

Currant leaf

CURRANTS AND GOOSEBERRIES
Ribes spp.

Use: The fruits are eaten raw, dried, or cooked/processed into juice, jam, and jelly.

Range: Species are found in the mountains, in the chaparral, in flat plains, along rivers, etc.

Similarity to toxic species: When seeing currants for the first time, some folks think they're looking at poison oak—they've heard the saying "leaflets 3, let it be." But the currant has 3 lobes per leaf, not 3 distinct leaflets as does poison oak.

Best time: The fruits are available in mid-spring.

Status: Common locally

Tools needed: Container for the fruit

Ripe golden currants. Note leaf shape, and note dried flower adhering to end of fruit.

Properties

Currants and gooseberries are both the same genus, and therefore we'll treat them together. Both are low shrubs with mostly long, vining shoots that arise from the base. Gooseberries have thorns on the stalks and fruits; currants do not.

The leaves look like little 3- to 5-fingered mittens. The fruits of both currants and gooseberries hang from the stalks, with the withered flower usually adhering to the end of the fruit.

You will find currants or gooseberries throughout the diverse ecosystems of California.

Uses

Though the straight shoots of the currants make excellent arrow shafts, currants and gooseberries are mostly regarded as a great fruit; they can be eaten as a snack, dried, or cooked into various recipes.

Gooseberries are a bit more work to eat because they're covered with tiny spines. I have mashed them all together and then strained the pulp through a sieve or fine colander, using it as a jelly for pancakes. Boy Scout leader Richard Toyon, a fourteenth-generation Californian descended from the Parra clan of the Acjachemen Nation, has reported that he found succulent gooseberries in the

Currant in fruit HELEN W. NYERGES

higher elevations of the Angeles National Forest, which his Boy Scouts mashed and used for pancake topping.

Currants require no preparation, and therefore they can be picked off the stalks and eaten fresh. However, make sure they are ripe; they'll be a bit tart otherwise.

In the old days, the currant was a valuable fruit; it was dried, powdered, and added to dried meats as a sugar preservative. Today you can just dry the fruits into simple trail snacks, or you can collect a lot and make jams, jellies, or even delicious drinks.

Moreover, though the currant leaf is not usually regarded as an important food source, some can be eaten in salads or cooked dishes for a bit of vitamin C. They are a bit tough as they get older, however.

Cautions
Be sure you've identified currant or gooseberry and that you can tell the difference between these and poison oak.

WALNUT FAMILY (JUGLANDACEAE)

The Walnut family contains 9 genera and about 60 species worldwide. In California, it is represented by the *Carya* genus (pecan) and the *Juglans* genus. There is only one member of *Carya,* which is *C. illinoinensis,* the introduced pecan tree, and it has now gone wild and often found in and near riparian areas. It is sometimes confused dwith the black walnut. *Juglans* is represented by 2 trees, the Northern California black walnut (*J. hindsii*) and the Southern California black walnut (*J. californica*).

Green unripe walnuts. Note the pinnately-divided leaves.

BLACK WALNUT
Juglans californica and *J. hindsii*

Use: The nutmeat is eaten. The green walnuts are used as fish stunner, and the black hulls are used for a dye.

Range: Common in lower-elevation canyons and valleys

Similarity to toxic species: None

Best time: Nuts mature in mid- to late summer.

Status: Common

Tools needed: Gloves suggested

Properties

In California, there are 2 native species of *Juglans,* as well as the introduced English walnut.

The black walnut is widespread in California's canyons, valleys, and hillsides. There are 2 species that might be encountered: *J. californica,* the Southern California black walnut, and *J. hindsii,* the Northern California black walnut. Additionally, you may encounter the English walnut (*J. regia*), either planted in yards or surviving around old farms and cabins.

This is a full-bodied native deciduous tree with pinnately divided leaves. There are typically 11–19 leaflets per leaf.

You know what the English walnut that you buy in the store looks like; this one is similar, but there are some important differences. First, all the black walnuts are smaller. They have a soft, green outer layer, which turns black as it matures and has long been used as a dye. The shell of the English walnut is thin and easy to crack, but approximately one-half of our black walnut is shell, and it requires a rock or a hammer to crack. The meat in the black walnut is oily and delicious, though there's not as much meat as you'll find in the cultivated English walnut.

A mature black walnut on the tree

Ripe walnuts cracked in a stone *molcajete*. Note that there is more shell than meat.

Uses

Yes, these are walnuts! However, unlike the more commonly cultivated English walnut, these black walnuts are more similar to the hickory nuts of eastern states.

Black walnuts are covered in a fleshy material that dries when the walnuts are mature and fall to the ground. This outer black covering is an excellent dye or pigment material for arts and crafts, but you want to consider wearing gloves when collecting. I once used this to paint lines and symbols on children's faces and arms at a day camp, and because the dye takes about 2 weeks to wash off, I heard from several unhappy parents.

Once you crack open the walnut, you can pick out the edible meat and eat it as is, or add it to bread products, cookies, cakes, and even stews and meat dishes. It is a very tasty, oil-rich food, and it is quite a delicacy, but it takes a lot of work to get to it.

The immature green walnuts were one of the substances used in the old days to capture fish. The local indigenous people would crush the green walnuts and toss them into pools of water or the edges of slow-moving streams, which would lead to the fish floating to the top. The fish would be scooped out with nets, and then everyone would have dinner!

MINT FAMILY (LAMIACEAE)

The Mint family has about 230 genera and about 7,200 species worldwide. In California, we have examples from 25 genera of the Mint family, many of which are used for food and medicine.

Wild mint JEFF MARTIN

MINT
Mentha spp.

Use: As a beverage and medicine
Range: Along rivers and wet areas; often cultivated
Similarity to toxic species: None
Best time: Mint can be collected anytime.
Status: Common locally, in the wild in and near streams
Tools needed: None

Properties

Of our 12 wild mints in California, only 1 is a native. In the wild, mints are typically found along streams. They are sprawling, vining plants with squarish stems and opposite, finely wrinkled leaves. Crush the leaf for the unmistakable clue to identification. If you have a good sense of smell, you'll detect the obvious minty aroma.

Peppermint, pennyroyal, spearmint, and *M. suaveolens* (sometimes called apple mint) are found in California but are usually cultivated in gardens. They sometimes escape cultivation and are found in marshy areas, moist areas, ditches, around lakes, and in meadows.

The white, pink, or violet flowers are clustered in tight groups along the stalk, often appearing like balls on the stems.

The flowers, though 5 petaled, consist of an upper 2-lobed section and a lower 3-lobed section.

Uses

Not primarily a food, the wild mints are excellent sources for an infused tea. Put your fresh leaves into your cup or pot, boil your water, and then pour the water over the leaves. Cover the cup and let it steep a bit. I enjoy the infusion plain, but you might prefer to add honey, lemon, or some other flavor.

Mint tea is often considered the tea of choice when you need to soothe the stomach.

We've had some campouts where we had very little food and relied on fishing and foraged food. Even during off-seasons in the mountains, we were able to find wild mint and make a refreshing tea. The aroma is invigorating and helps to open the sinuses. To me, the flavor and taste of mint tea seems even more enjoyable when camping. Also, you can just crush some fresh leaves and add them to your canteen while hiking. It makes a great, cold trail beverage and requires no sweeteners.

Sometimes we add the fresh leaves to trout while it is cooking. It adds a great flavor.

If used sparingly, you can dice up the fresh leaves and add them to salads for a refreshing minty flavor. Of course, they can be diced and added to various dessert dishes, like ice cream, sherbet, and so on. Alternatively, you can try adding a few sprigs of mint to your soups and stews to liven up the flavor. And if you really want to try something special for your doomsday parties, add a little fresh mint to your favorite pouch of MREs.

Chia plant HELEN W. NYERGES

CHIA
Salvia columbariae

Use: Primarily, the seeds are used in drinks and other foods.
Range: Prefers the desert flats but can be found in other environments
Similarity to toxic species: None
Best time: Seeds mature around early July.
Status: Somewhat common locally in a good season
Tools needed: A tight-weave bag

Properties
Though there are about 900 species of *Salvia* in the world, only 19 (not counting varieties) are found in California. Of these, 17 species are native and generally go by some variation of the name "sage." The leaves of most *Salvias* are prized for

Chia leaf RICK ADAMS

spice and medicine, and the seeds of all are edible. The *Salvias* are also a valuable plant for bees.

Chia prefers desert flats, and that's where you'll find it in the greatest abundance. However, you can also find it in many other zones, such as in the chaparral, typically where the soil has been disturbed, and even in higher elevations in the mountains up to about 4,000'. Not only that, it's relatively easy to cultivate down in the coastal desert plains and in backyards.

The plant is an obvious mint, with its square stem and opposite leaves that are finely divided and creased. The flower also is a typical mint, with pale to deep blue flowers

A view of the growing chia plant

that are formed in whorls (appearing like balls) along the stalk.

The tiny gray to tan seeds mature around July, when the seed balls mature and turn tan.

Uses

The golden chia seeds are legendary in Indian lore and history, and they were first recorded by Dr. J. T. Rothrock, who was both a botanist and surgeon for the Wheeler US Geological Survey in 1875. He wrote that "one tablespoon of these seeds was sufficient to sustain for 24 hours an Indian on a forced march." (He was referring to the runners and traders who could get by on just the chia seeds if they had nothing else.)

In fact, the seeds are an easily digestible form of protein, and—though not everyone agrees with me—I think they taste good, too! I add them to coffee, fruit drinks, and water. I mix them into yogurt, cottage cheese, and sour cream. I toss the seeds in cereals, salads, soups, and omelets. I have even ground them and added them to batter for breads and pancakes. Chia seeds also can be combined with chopped dates and figs and pounded into a high-protein "nutrition bar."

I was heavily influenced by Harrison Doyle's book on chia, *Golden Chia: Ancient Indian Energy Food.* I learned that the common chia sold in health food stores is typically not the *S. columbariae* seeds used by the desert Indians but rather *S. hispanica.* If you really enjoy native chia seeds and don't have a way to grow them yourself, keep in mind that the nutritional content of the native *S. columbariae* and *S. hispanica* are similar, so you're still getting a good food with the chia seeds from the health food store.

A view of the cultivated "health food store" chia (left) and the native golden chia seed (right)

MALLOW FAMILY (MALVACEAE)

The Mallow family includes 266 genera and about 4,025 species worldwide. There are 18 genera represented in California, including *Hibiscus*. According to Dr. Leonid Enari, the Mallow family is safe for wild food experimentation. He cautions, however, that some species may be too fibrous to eat.

Mallow leaves

MALLOW
Malva neglecta

Use: Leaves raw, cooked, or dried (for tea); "cheeses" eaten raw or cooked; seeds cooked and eaten like rice

Range: Urban areas such as fields, disturbed soils, gardens

Similarity to toxic species: None

Best time: Spring

Status: Common and widespread

Tools needed: None

Properties

There are 30–40 species of *Malva* worldwide. In California, there are 7, but only 1 is a native.

The plants resemble geraniums with their rounded leaves. Each leaf's margin is finely toothed, and there is a cleft to the middle of the leaf to which the long stem is attached. If you look closely, you'll see a red spot where the stem meets the leaf.

The flowers are small but attractive, composed of 5 petals, generally colored white to blue, though some could be lilac or pink. These flowers are followed by the round flat fruits, which gave rise to its other name, "cheeseweed."

These are indeed widespread, mostly in the urban terrain and on the fringes. In the desert and other areas of California, there are other related genera of the Mallow family, such as the bush mallow (*Malacothamnus* sp.) and the checker mallow (*Sidalcea* sp.).

Uses

When you take a raw leaf and chew on it, you will find it a bit mucilaginous. For this reason, it is used to soothe a sore throat. In Mexico, you can find the dried leaf under the Spanish name *malva* at herb stores, sold as a medicine. In this form, it is

Mallow with round seed clusters

typically made into an infusion for sore throats and coughs.

Though the entire plant is edible, the stalks and leaf stems tend to be a bit fibrous. Therefore, I just use the leaf and discard the stem. These are good added to salads, though they are a bit tough as the only salad ingredient.

The mallow leaf is also good in any cooked dishes—soups, stews, or chopped up fine for omelets and stir-fries.

I have even seen some attempts to substitute the larger mallow leaves for grape leaves in dolma, which is cooked rice wrapped in a grape leaf. I thought it worked out pretty well.

As this plant flowers and matures, the flat and round seed clusters appear. When still green, these make a good nibble. These

Mallow seeds

green "cheeses" (as they are commonly called) can be added raw to salads, cooked in soups, or even pickled into capers. Once the plant is fully mature and the leaves are drying up, you can collect the now-mature cheeses. The round clusters will break up into individual seeds, which you can winnow and then cook similar to rice. Though the cooked seeds are a bit bland, they are reminiscent of rice. Because mallow is so very common, it would not be hard to prepare a dish of the mallow seed. To really improve the flavor, try mixing the mallow seeds with quinoa, buckwheat groats, or couscous.

The root of the related marsh mallow (*Althaea officinalis*) was once used for making marshmallow, which is now just another junk food. Originally, the roots were boiled until the water was gelatinous. The water would be whipped to thicken it and then sweetened. You'd then have a spoonful to treat a cough or sore throat. Yes, you can use the common mallow's roots to try this, though it doesn't get quite as thick as the original.

MINER'S LETTUCE FAMILY (MONTIACEAE)

The Miner's Lettuce family includes 22 genera, with about 230 species world-wide. There are 6 genera represented in California. Dr. Leonid Enari regarded this as a completely safe family for wild food experimentation. He taught that all members could be eaten, usually raw but sometimes needing to be steamed or cooked for improved palatability. Dr. Enari also taught that the seeds of most could be harvested and eaten.

Miner's lettuce amid the grass RICK ADAMS

MINER'S LETTUCE
Claytonia perfoliata

Use: Entire aboveground plant can be eaten raw, boiled, steamed, sautéed, or added to soup, eggs, etc.
Range: Mostly found in moist canyons below 3,000'
Similarity to toxic species: None
Best time: Spring
Status: Common seasonally
Tools needed: None

Properties

There are 27 species of *Claytonia* worldwide. There are 14 species found in California (not including subspecies); all are native.

Miner's lettuce was one of the very first wild foods that I learned to identify. I'd seen the characteristic leaf—a round, cuplike leaf with the flower stalk growing out of the middle—in Bradford Angier's book *Free for the Eating*. It was just one drawing, but I was certain I'd be able to recognize it. One day I got a phone call from a fellow budding forager, and he told me that he'd spotted the plant about 1,000' up an incline in the local mountains. I biked to the site that day and climbed up the hillside, and sure enough, I found it!

That night, I tried my first miner's lettuce in salad and boiled some like spinach. It was good, but perhaps the experience was a bit anticlimactic because I was so wrapped up in the lore and history of the plant. I didn't realize there'd be nothing really incredible about the plant—just a tasty though somewhat bland leaf that could be used in many ways.

Miner's lettuce leaves are formed in a rosette, with each leaf arising from the root. The young leaves are linear, and the older ones are somewhat triangular to quadrangular in shape, with some appearing water-spotted. The key characteristic is the flowering stalk with its pink or white 5-petaled flowers, which arise from a cup-shaped leaf. Clusters of these unique leaves, all arising from a common root, like a head of leaf lettuce, make this a very easy plant to recognize.

Uses

It seems that everyone in California knows miner's lettuce. This is probably because the plant is so distinctive—when it's in flower, you really can't confuse it with something else. Plus, it tastes good, it often grows very abundantly, and it's

Miner's lettuce in flower RICK ADAMS

Miner's lettuce. Note how the flower stalk grows through the round leaf. RICK ADAMS

easy to work with. Think of the plant as a somewhat succulent lettuce that is also good cooked, and you'll get some idea how versatile this plant can be.

Flavor- and texture-wise, this is perhaps one of my favorite wild foods. My brother, Richard, always regarded it as his favorite. We have used it in many recipes—just think of all the diverse ways in which we use common spinach!

To give some examples of the many ways in which we can eat miner's lettuce, consider a weekend survival trip I once led for a dozen young men. Our only food was what we fished or foraged, and there was very little growing in the area besides miner's lettuce, along with a small amount of mustard. We had miner's lettuce salad, miner's lettuce soup, fried miner's lettuce, boiled miner's lettuce, miner's lettuce cooked with fish, and miner's lettuce broth! If we were in a kitchen with all sorts of condiments, we'd have had miner's lettuce omelets, soufflés, stir-fries, and green drinks.

In other words, in any recipe that calls for greens—raw, cooked, or juiced—you can use miner's lettuce.

RECIPE

Richard's Salad

4 cups rinsed miner's lettuce leaves

Dressing of equal parts olive oil (cold-pressed) and raw apple cider vinegar, to which he added a dash of garlic powder and paprika, to taste

—RECIPE FROM MY BROTHER, RICHARD, WHO MADE MINER'S LETTUCE SALADS WHENEVER POSSIBLE IN THE SPRING

OXALIS FAMILY (OXALIDACEAE)

Though the Oxalis family contains 5 genera and 880 species worldwide, in California, it is represented only by the *Oxalis* genus. There are 10 species of *Oxalis* in California.

Typical *Oxalis* leaf: three heart-shaped segments joined at the apex

SOUR GRASS / WOOD SORREL
Oxalis spp.

Use: Everything can be used. Aboveground leaves and stems can be used raw, cooked, or pickled. The tiny tubers can also be cooked and eaten.
Range: Some are very common in the urban setting, and others are found in mountains, meadows, and fields.
Similarity to toxic species: None
Best time: Generally spring
Status: Common in urban areas
Tools needed: None

Properties
Sour grass is widespread, and most gardeners hate it because it is such a successful plant. It spreads and spreads, and if it grows in your yard, there's probably much

more than you're likely to use for food. This is one of the plants commonly referred to as a shamrock, or four-leaf clover. However, *Oxalis* is not a clover and is not related to clover.

The leaves arise from thin stems, and each leaf appears to be 3 hearts connected at the apex of those hearts (though you will occasionally find 4 leaflets). Many leaves appear to be water-spotted. The flower stalks are typically taller than the leaves. For example, on the common *O. pes-caprae,* regarded as a noxious pest by urban gardeners, the flower stalk with its yellow flowers is significantly taller and slightly thicker. The flower stalk of *O. pes-caprae* can rise up to 1', especially in urban gardens.

Wood sorrel (*O. pes-caprae*) in flower

The flower colors vary from species to species, from white, to pink, to yellow.

If you dig around under the plant, you'll see some of the tiny tubers of the plant, typically no bigger than a pea.

FORAGER'S NOTE: Though the little tubers underneath the California Oxalis plants are very small, there is a variety called oca (*O. tuberosa*) that has long been cultivated in its native Peru, Bolivia, and Ecuador. These tubers measure just a few inches and are very acidic when fresh. They are dried in the sun for a few days to improve the flavor. When they are dried for a few weeks, the flavor is said to resemble figs. Therefore, at the very least, when you see the little tubers under the California species, you can try them as a nibble or experiment with cooking or drying them.

Uses

Yes, this makes a good trail nibble, but you really can't eat a lot—it's just too sour because of the plant's oxalic acid. However, everyone likes this plant. Children rarely refuse sour grass. It's a great snack, and it livens up other foods.

Use the leaves sparingly in salads for a vinegar flavor. I prefer the flower stalks, but everything aboveground can be used.

Everything aboveground can also be cooked into soups or stews, but, again, add it sparingly. If it's a bit too strong, boil the plant, rinse the water, and then use.

I've had some fermented sour grass that was made just as you'd make sauerkraut with cabbage. Though it was very stringy, it was still tasty.

Cautions

Remember, use the stems and leaves from this plant sparingly. Consuming these on an empty stomach could result in vomiting.

PASSIONFLOWER FAMILY (PASSIFLORACEAE)

The Passionflower family consists of 17 genera and 750 species worldwide. In California, this family is represented only by the *Passiflora* genus.

The unique passion flower RICK ADAMS

PASSIONFLOWER
Passiflora caerulea and *P. tarminiana*

Use: Fruits eaten raw or processed into jams, etc.; leaves and flowers for a medicinal tea
Range: Urban areas, around riparian areas, often invasive; doesn't survive freezing
Similarity to toxic species: None
Best time: Fruit is available in early to midsummer; leaves can be gathered year-round.
Status: Common and invasive in certain areas
Tools needed: None

Properties
Though there are 540 reported species of *Passiflora* worldwide, there are only 2 wild species in California. Many varieties are grown in gardens.

Both of our wild California passionflowers are native to South America. They are a good source of food and medicine and also reportedly have served as a mnemonic tool to teach about the Passion of the Christ.

The vining plant can be seen trailing over bushes and trees, and then the fruits will be seen hanging from these bushes. The leaves are palmately divided like a hand, and the tendrils help the plant grab onto other vegetation.

Some people are shocked when they see passionflower for the first time, thinking it is some plastic invention. It has what looks like 10 petals, but actually it has 5 sepals and 5 identical petals. There is a colorful purple ring called the corolla. The 5 stamens are outstretched evenly, and right in the middle is a 3-part pistil. It's all very colorful, and it's hard to believe that such a flower exists in all of nature.

Ripe fruit of the passionflower hanging from the vine

RECIPE

Lemon and Wild Passion Fruit Marmalade

The recipe is very simple and truly delicious.

2 cups passion fruit (*Passiflora caerulea*) with skin and seeds

3 cups sugar

2 whole large lemons, diced (skin and pulp)

1 teaspoon cinnamon

Place all the ingredients into a pot, bring to a boil, and stir from time to time. Supervise until the solution reaches the exact temperature of 220°F.

Pour into jars, close the lids, and place in the fridge.

If you know how to can, use the water-bath method for 15 minutes.

—RECIPE FROM PASCAL BAUDAR

The egg-size fruits begin green and ripen by summer into an orange fruit with red, seedy insides, which is the main edible portion.

Uses

Passionflower fruit matures in early summer, with the orange egg-shaped fruits hanging from the plant's vines in the willows and oaks and whatever trees the vine is growing on. Split open the ripe fruit and eat the red seeds. It's a little mucilaginous and sweet but not overly sweet. It makes a good trail snack. I enjoy them while hiking, as well as chilled and eaten out of hand.

I've had fruit leather made from the red seeds, crushed and laid flat on a cookie pan until it dried. It had a good texture, and the flavor was improved by drying. This is a great way to make food for storage and for trips.

The fruit also makes a good jam or jelly, usually with a bit of honey added. You can brew the red seeds into a tasty drink, though, again, it's improved with a dash of honey.

The leaves are often infused into a tea, though they have a very mild flavor, so mint or other aromatic herbs can be added. The herb contains a very weak sedative, and if you have trouble getting to sleep, this is just the tea for a bedtime drink.

LOPSEED FAMILY (PHRYMACEAE)

The Lopseed family contains 15 genera worldwide, with 230 species. In California, *Mimulus* is the only genus representing this family. (*Mimulus* had formerly been classified in the Figwort family.)

Monkey flower in bloom HELEN W. NYERGES

COMMON MIMULUS (YELLOW MONKEY FLOWER)
Mimulus guttatus

Use: Everything tender above the waterline
Range: Always found in slow-moving waters or ponds
Similarity to toxic species: None
Best time: Spring
Status: Common in some areas, not particularly widespread
Tools needed: None

Properties
Members of the *Mimulus* genus are generally referred to as monkey flowers. There are about 100 species worldwide, with 62 species in California, all of which are natives.

This is a common yellow wild-flower that grows along the shallow banks of streams, in much the same environment as watercress. It's usually very conspicuous when in flower and fairly easy to recognize.

The bright yellow flowers are typically on a raceme, with 5 or so flowers per stalk. The flower is composed of an upper lip with 2 lobes and a lower lip with 3 lobes, which also may have many red to brown spots or just one large spot. The opening to the tubular flower is hairy.

The plant may be an annual or perennial, with the stems either

A good view of the flower LILY JANE TSONG

erect or sprawling in the water. It's a highly variable plant.

The leaves are opposite, round to oval in shape, usually with irregular teeth.

Uses

Because the common monkey flower grows in slow-moving waters, make sure that the water is clean if you plan to use it in salads.

I've used the leaves and tender stems in salads many times, and I just pinch off the tender above-water sections. The texture is good, and the flavor is mild, so it makes a good addition to salads, either alone or mixed with a variety of other wild greens for a balanced flavor. Add some tomatoes and avocado, too. Of course, I nearly always add salad dressing to make it tasty.

The greens also lend themselves well to various cooked dishes. You can simply boil them like spinach, or you can try stir-frying them with other greens and vegetables.

The entire plant of the common monkey flower is mild and can go into any soup or stew pot.

A view of the flower and leaf of the yellow monkey flower LILY JANE TSONG

PLANTAIN FAMILY (PLANTAGINACEAE)

The Plantain family has 110 genera and approximately 2,000 species worldwide. There are 26 genera in California.

Veronica in a bed of watercress

VERONICA (AKA SPEEDWELL)
Veronica americana

Use: The entire plant (tender stems and leaves) above the root
Range: Grows in slow-moving waters in the same environment as watercress
Similarity to toxic species: None
Best time: Spring and summer
Status: Somewhat common
Tools needed: None

Properties
The *Veronica* genus has about 250 species worldwide, 11 of which are found in California; of those, 7 are native and 4 are introduced.

V. americana is a native and is frequently confused with watercress because they both grow in water. I admit to the superficial resemblance, but there really are some obvious differences. The veronica has a simple leaf about 1"–2" long, whereas the watercress has pinnately divided leaves very much like many of the members of the Mustard family. The watercress has a typical mustard flower formula with the 4 petals arranged similar to a cross, and its color is white. However, the veronica flower is lavender and asymmetrical with 4 petals, with the upper petal being wider than the others.

Veronica flower RICK ADAMS

Uses

If I have no concerns about the water's safety from which I've picked the veronica, I add it to salads. It is not strongly flavored, and you can use the entire plant. Just pinch it off at water level (no need to uproot the plant), rinse it, and then dice it into your salad. No need to pick off just the leaves—eat the entire above-water plant.

Because it's so bland, you can mix it with stronger-flavored greens in your salad. It goes well with watercress, as well as any of the mustards.

Veronica goes well with soup dishes and stir-fries. It never gets strongly bitter, like watercress, and it never really gets fibrous. It's a mild plant that's fairly widespread in waterways.

If you live near a waterway where veronica grows, you'll find that it's a good plant to use in a variety of dishes where you might otherwise include spinach. Try some gently sautéed with green onions, add some eggs, and make an omelet. Or try a cream soup into which you've gently cooked some of the veronica greens.

Young veronica in streambed RICK ADAMS

BUCKWHEAT FAMILY (POLYGONACEAE)

The Buckwheat family has 48 genera and about 1,200 species worldwide; 27 of these genera are found in California. Of the 250 known species of *Eriogonum* found worldwide, 119 are found in California, not counting the many varieties.

Buckwheat with mature flowers

CALIFORNIA BUCKWHEAT
Eriogonum fasciculatum

Use: Seed heads are used for flour (such as for pancakes or porridge).

Range: Chaparral zone mostly, fringes of the desert

Similarity to toxic species: None

Best time: Harvest the seeds from approximately August through February.

Status: Widespread within its niche

Tools needed: Bucket or bag

Properties

In the California chaparral region and in parts of the desert, you will find this buckwheat growing prolifically. The plant forms low bushes with its rosemary-like leaves, though the edges of the California buckwheat are rolled over on the edges. While the leaf is nearly identical in size to rosemary's needlelike leaf, there is none of the sweet fragrance of rosemary. In the spring, the plant sends up flower stalks with flowers formed in what appears to be a ball. The flowers balls are white in the spring; by summer, the seeds ripen, and the balls turn a shade of chocolate brown.

Of California's 119 species of *Eriogonum,* this species of buckwheat is the most abundant in seed. It is the most common overall, and contains seeds that are easily harvested.

Uses

Buckwheat is an amazing grain. It is abundant in the fall and requires no leaching to produce meal from it. The seed heads are easily harvested in the fall when they are ripe. Just use your hand to pick them off and place in a bucket or bag. Where the plant grows thickly, it is not difficult to collect 5 gallons of the seed heads in under an hour.

I used to try winnowing out the seeds from the wings surrounding them. This proved to be a lot of work to rub them between the hands to free the seed and then to gently blow off the chaff. While researching how the California Native Americans

Buckwheat with the new white flowers of spring

processed the buckwheat, I learned that winnowing was not the norm, so then my processing became a lot easier. I just collect the seed heads, rub them between my hands to produce a coarse meal, pick out the stems, and then mix this 50-50 with conventional flours. I use this mix to produce bread, biscuits, pancakes, and cookies.

Botanical Note

California Buckwheat is not the same as the commonly cultivated buckwheat (*Fagopyrum esculentum*). They are both, however, in the same Buckwheat family, and each is a member of a different genus. Neither buckwheat is related to wheat, nor is either a grass.

The wild ancestor of the common buckwheat can be traced back to about 4000 BC to the Yunnan Province located in southwestern China.

Immature dock seed stalk

CURLY DOCK
Rumex crispus

Use: Young dock leaves used raw or cooked; seeds harvested and added to various flours; stems used like rhubarb

Range: Prefers wet areas but can be found in most environments

Similarity to toxic species: None

Best time: The leaves are best gathered when young in the spring. Seeds mature in late August and may be available for months.

Status: Common and widespread

Tools needed: None

Properties

Rumex has between 190 and 200 species worldwide; 23 are found in California, 15 of which are native—but not curly dock.

Curly dock is a widespread, invasive perennial plant in most of California. It is originally from Europe, and though it has many good uses, it is often despised and poisoned because it not only survives well but also often takes over entire areas.

The root looks similar to an orange carrot, and the spring leaves arise directly from the root. The young leaves are long and linear and are curved on their margins. The leaves can be over 1' long and pointed.

As the season progresses, the flower stalk arises, and it can reach about 4' or even taller in ideal

Mature dock seed stalk

conditions. Three seeds, each surrounded by a papery sheath, form each unit. They are green at first and then mature to a beautiful chocolate brown.

Uses

You can make various dishes from both the leaves and the mature seeds of curly dock. Let's start with the leaves.

Pick only the very youngest leaves for salad, the smaller ones before the plant has begun to send up its seed stalk. These will not be too tough, and the flavor will be sour, somewhat like French sorrel. You can just rinse them, dice them, and add them to salads. I've had *only* these for salads, with dressing and avocado, and they were good but only because the leaves were young.

Older leaves are best boiled like spinach, or—ideally with the midrib removed—sautéed with potatoes and onions. You can also add some to soups and stews. The leaves change color and darken a bit upon cooking, and the cooking softens up the tougher, older leaves, but you really want to cook the

Christopher with a perfect example of dock leaves RICK ADAMS

tougher, bitter, and astringent older leaves. All these qualities are reduced somewhat by cooking.

I have seen the brown seed spikes sold in floral supply shops as fall decoration, and they are very attractive. Those little seeds can be stripped off the stalks and then rubbed between your hands to remove the wing from the seed. You don't have to be too picky here, as it can all be used. I blow off the wings and then mix the seed 50-50 with flour for pancakes and sometimes bread. You could also toss some seed into soup to increase the protein content.

I've seen some folks who go to the trouble of winnowing and then further grinding the seeds in a mill to get fine flour. I never bother, but some folks prefer the finer flour, which is a bit more versatile than the seeds. For example, a fine flour can be mixed 50-50 with wheat, blended, and put through a pasta machine to make a curly dock–seed pasta, which tastes really good.

The stems are tart and sour, but often they make a good nibble. Young stems can be processed and used similar to rhubarb for pies.

Curly Dock "Nori" (Vegetable Chips)

Dehydration is a neat way to make some interesting and flavorful ingredients for wild food dishes. This one is easy to do. You will just need a silicone sheet.

100 g (about 3.5 oz) chopped curly dock

1 garlic clove

½ cup water

2 teaspoons soy sauce

¼ teaspoon salt

Blend everything and, using a spatula, spread it on a silicone sheet.
Dehydrate at 160°F until fully dry.

—RECIPE FROM PASCAL BAUDAR

Caution

Since curly dock can be a persistent, unwanted plant in agricultural areas, herbicides are sometimes used to combat it. Be careful, use common sense, and ask questions before collecting curly dock from agricultural areas.

Sheep sorrel GARY GONZALEZ

SHEEP SORREL
Rumex acetosella

Use: The raw leaves are good in salads and can also be added to various cooked dishes.
Range: Found in the higher elevations, often around water, and frequently near disturbed soils and in urban areas
Similarity to toxic species: None
Best time: Spring to early summer
Status: Can be abundant locally
Tools needed: None

Properties
Sheep sorrel is not native to California but is to Europe and Asia.

Sheep sorrel is common and widespread, and the plant is recognized by its characteristic leaves, which are generally basal, lance to oblong shaped, with a hastate- or sagittate-tapered base; in other words, it looks similar to an elongated arrowhead. When the seed stalk matures, it is brown and reminiscent of the curly dock seed stalk but much smaller.

Uses

Where the plant is common, you can pinch off many of the small leaves to add to salad or even to use as the main ingredient in salad. I've enjoyed sheep sorrel salads with just avocado and dressing added. The leaves are mildly sour, making a very tangy salad.

The flavor is somewhat similar to the leaves of *Oxalis,* though not as strong. They can be effectively added raw to other foods such as tostadas (in place of lettuce) or in sandwiches.

They add a bit of a tang when added to soups and stews, and they can be very effective at livening up some MREs.

Sheep sorrel LOUIS-M. LANDRY

RECIPE

Shiyo's Garden Salad

Rinse a bowlful of young sheep sorrel leaves. Add at least 1 ripe avocado and 1 ripe tomato, both diced. Add some oil-and-vinegar dressing; my preference is Dr. Bronner's. Eat it outside where the wind can blow your hair.

Wild rhubarb

WILD RHUBARB
Rumex hymenosepalus

Use: The youngest leaves and stems are used in salads, older leaves can be cooked, and stems used like rhubarb.
Range: Most common in the Mojave Desert, but found in low valleys and chaparral regions as well
Similarity to toxic species: None
Best time: Spring
Status: Not widespread; appears singly or in patches
Tools needed: None

Properties
This plant is also known as canaigre. Though this plant seems to largely be restricted to the low and high deserts, it does grow outside such zones on occasion. If you know curly dock (*R. crispus*), which is actually found worldwide, you will automatically assume you're looking at curly dock when you see the wild rhubarb for the first time. However, wild rhubarb doesn't just spread its seed and grow *everywhere,* as does the dock; you will typically find patches of wild rhubarb here and there. Sometimes you'll encounter isolated patches.

The leaves look similar to the wavy leaf of curly dock, but they are not as linear as the dock. Wild rhubarb leaves are wavy on the margins, but they are more of a dull green color, and the width might be half the overall length of the leaf (where a curly dock leaf may be 5 to 6 times as long as it is wide).

The stems are stout and succulent, and the mature flower spikes resemble those of curly dock, though they are not as tall as the curly dock spike.

Uses

In general, you can think of the uses of wild rhubarb as the same as curly dock, but wild rhubarb generally contains more oxalic acid. This means it's more sour and more bitter and thus requires more cooking to make it palatable.

Wild rhubarb beginning to flower

You might disregard this altogether, thinking it's too much work, but in some parts of the desert, wild rhubarb is one of the few common plants that you can use to make a meal.

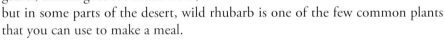

Gently boil the stems and the leaves (separately or together) and change the water. When they are no longer too bitter and are palatable, you can use them in soups, stews, sautéed dishes, or simply served with butter, cheese, or other seasonings.

I've had "rhubarb" pie made with just the stems of this plant and liked it more than garden rhubarb. However, just like garden rhubarb, cooks usually add way too much sugar to make rhubarb pie. Health-oriented cooks can tweak the recipe just so and use honey to create an excellent, healthful pie. By the way, it makes a green pie, not a red pie like garden rhubarb.

The seeds could also be collected when mature and then ground and added to soup or pancake batter, as you could also do with the seeds of curly dock. Try it sparingly at first, as the seeds are a bit stronger in flavor than those of curly dock.

PURSLANE FAMILY (PORTULACACEAE)

The Purslane family has recently been redefined by botanists as having only 1 genus, with about 100 species worldwide, and only 2 members of that genus are found in California. This family (which once had many more members—now classified in the Miner's Lettuce family) was considered by Dr. Leonid Enari to be entirely safe for consumption.

Young purslane

PURSLANE
Portulaca oleracea

DESERT PORTULACA
P. halimoides

Use: Entire aboveground plant can be used raw, cooked, pickled, etc.

Range: Prefers disturbed soils of gardens and rose beds; also found in the sandy areas around rivers

Similarity to toxic species: Somewhat resembles prostrate spurge; however, spurge lacks the succulence of purslane. Also, when you break the stem of spurge, a white milky sap appears.

Best time: Spring into summer

Status: Relatively common
Tools needed: None

Properties

Purslane starts appearing a bit later than most of the spring greens, typically by June or July. It is a very common annual in rose beds and gardens, though I do see it in the wild occasionally, typically in the sandy bottoms around streams.

Young purslane

The stems are succulent, red colored, and round in the cross section. The stems sprawl outward from the roots, rosette-like, with the stems lying on the ground. The leaves are paddle shaped. The little yellow flower is 5 petaled.

If you know purslane, you'll probably recognize the similarity to desert portulaca in the sandy washes and open flats. The leaves are succulent, like purslane, but more elongated. The flower petals are red. You'll only see this one in the spring following wet winters. Also, desert portulaca is nowhere near as common as purslane.

Note the red stem and paddle-shaped leaves of purslane.

Uses

When you chew on a fresh stem or leaf of purslane, you'll find it mildly sour and a bit crunchy. It's really a great snack, though I like it a lot in salads. Just rinse it to get all the dirt off, dice, add some dressing, and serve. Yes, add tomatoes and avocado if you have any.

Add it to sandwiches, tostadas, even on the edges of your chiles rellenos and huevos rancheros. I've also eaten it fried, boiled, baked (in egg dishes), and probably other ways, too. It's versatile, tasty, and crisp. It really goes with anything, and it's very nutritious.

If you take the thick stems, clean off the leaves, and cut them into sections of about 4", you can make purslane pickles. There are many ways to make pickles; my way is to simply fill the jar with the purslane stems, add raw apple cider vinegar, and let it sit for a few weeks. (I refrigerate it.)

Medicinal Properties

According to researchers, purslane is one of the richest plant sources of omega-3 fatty acids. That means that not only is it good but it's also good for you!

RECIPE

Purslane Salsa

2 cups chopped tomatoes

2½ cups chopped foraged purslane

¾ cup chopped onions

3 garlic cloves

1 cup raw apple cider vinegar

¼ cup sugar

1 large California bay leaf

Salt and pepper to taste

½ cup chopped cilantro and some herbs from the garden (such as thyme)

Place all ingredients, except cilantro and other herbs, into a pot, bring to a boil, and then simmer to the desired consistency (light or chunky). Add cilantro and other herbs.

Pour into jars, close the lids, and place in the fridge. It should be good for at least a month.

—RECIPE FROM PASCAL BAUDAR

BUCKTHORN FAMILY (RHAMNACEAE)

There are 50–52 genera of the Buckthorn family worldwide, with about 950 species.

Coffee berry with immature fruits

CALIFORNIA COFFEE BERRY
Frangula californica and *F. purshiana*

Use: Seeds used for a beverage; bark for laxative
Range: Chaparral and coastal ranges
Similarity to toxic species: None
Best time: Fruits mature in August and September.
Status: Scattered widely
Tools needed: None

Properties

There are 50 species of the *Frangula* genus, with 3 species found in California. *F. californica* and its 6 subspecies are most common in Southern California; *F. purshiana* and its 3 subspecies are found more commonly in the northern part of California. These are small shrubs to large trees, depending on location and species. *F. californica* is typically no more than 8' tall, whereas *F. purshiana* is significantly taller, very treelike. The leaves are alternately arranged, 1"–2" in length, typically bright green, and narrowly oblong with tiny teeth on the margins. The fruits are green and turn red before becoming nearly black as they mature. They are little globes up to ½" in diameter, with 2 and sometimes 3 seeds. The seeds closely resemble the seeds of commercial coffee.

Uses

You could pick a few of the nearly black ripe fruits around August and eat them as trail nibble, but don't eat too many. The plant is a known laxative, and the ripe fruit can have that effect.

Fruits, ripening

I have had some jam prepared from the ripe flesh of the coffee berry fruits. It was uniquely flavored; it didn't appeal to me, but some folks really love it.

Most of the time, it is the seeds of this plant that foragers collect. Harvest the fruit when mature. You could quickly squeeze the seeds out of each fruit—that's the long way. You could also just mush them all up between your hands to get all the fruit separated from the seed, wash it well, and then lay it in the sun to dry. When dry, you can further rub the seeds between the hands to get rid of all remaining flesh.

The seeds are then dried, ground, roasted, and percolated to make a caffeine-free, coffee-tasting beverage. It really smells like coffee, as well as more or less tasting like it. Serve it plain or with honey and cream, as with regular coffee. You could also use it as a coffee extender, mixing 50-50 with coffee.

Caution

Try this beverage sparingly at first; a small percentage of people will vomit after trying it.

Coffee berry with green fruit RICK ADAMS

ROSE FAMILY (ROSACEAE)

The Rose family contains 110 genera and around 3,000 species worldwide. Species from 45 of the genera are found in California.

Green fruit of the toyon RICK ADAMS

TOYON
Heteromeles arbutifolia

Use: Berries cooked, dried, or made into flour
Range: Chaparral hillsides; sometimes cultivated
Similarity to toxic species: Somewhat resembles European holly fruits
Best time: Fruits mature from about October through January.
Status: Common
Tools needed: None

Properties

The toyon is the only species of the *Heteromeles* genus. (*Heteromeles* is Greek for "different apple.")

Toyon can grow to a medium-size tree and is probably most conspicuous in the winter, when it's covered with its clusters of orange-red fruits, which are pomes.

The tree is found in the chaparral zones and often planted on the

The ripe toyon fruit cooked with a little honey, made into tarts

fringes of urban areas. The leaves are leathery and ovate, with toothed margins. The tree is evergreen and can be a large bush or a small- to medium-size tree.

In the summer, the flowers form in terminal clusters. Each flower is white, 5 petaled, and about ¼" wide. The clusters of orange-red fruit ripen from about November into January.

A cluster of the ripe toyon fruit

Uses

I have one Native American friend who likes to pick fresh toyon berries from the tree and eat them raw. He says he likes them, and I believe him; everyone has a different sense of taste. In general, I find them a bit too dry and astringent for a raw snack.

I prefer to collect a gallon or so of the fruit and roll them gently between my hands to remove all the stems. Then I put the berries into a dishpan with warm water and clean the fruit. Next, I dry them—in the sun or in the oven with just the pilot light on. The dry fruits then make a good nibble, or they can be used in a variety of ways: One is to grind the dry fruit into flour and add that flour to bread and pancake mixes. It adds a mild sweetness to the mix. You can add the dried toyon berries to wild-nut mixes or soak them in water a bit before adding them to bread or pancake batter. Alternatively, if you add the fresh berries to water, boil them gently, rinse the water, and add fresh water again, they can be eaten as is, sweetened, or added to other dishes.

A cider can also be made from these fruits. Clean and boil the fruits and sweeten to taste.

RECIPE

Chumash Winter

Boil 2 cups fresh toyon berries in water for a minute or so, and pour off the water. Add a little fresh water, and cook gently. Add 2 tablespoons honey and stir. Add some flour, stir, and cook until you have a thick dessert, with almost an oatmeal-like consistency.

Wild cherry leaf

WILD CHERRIES
Prunus spp.

Use: The flesh of the fruit in jams and jellies; process the meat of the large seed into a flour.
Range: Chaparral, coastal ranges, riparian, urban fringes
Similarity to toxic species: None
Best time: Fruits mature around August.
Status: Common
Tools needed: None

Properties

There are about 400 species of *Prunus* worldwide, whose common names generally include cherry, almond, apricot, and plum. In California, there are 11 species of *Prunus* (but we're only concerned with the cherries here). There are 4 wild cherries in California. The first 2 listed below are evergreen trees or

Ripe wild cherry

Ripe wild cherry fruits

bushes in California; the leaves are stiff and shiny, with teeth on the margins (depending on species). The second 2 are deciduous.

- Holly leaf cherry (*P. ilicifolia* subspecies *ilicifolia*)
- Catalina Island cherry (*P. ilicifolia* subspecies *lyonii*)
- Bitter cherry (*P. emarginata*)
- Western chokecherry (*P. virginiana* var. *demissa*)

One way to identify the plant is to crush the leaves, wait a few seconds, and then smell them. They will have a distinct aroma of bitter almond extract, your clue that the leaf contains cyanide (hydrocyanic acid).

The fruits are very much like cultivated cherries, except the color is darker red, almost maroon, sometimes even darker. The flesh layer can be very thin in dry years and thicker in the seasons following a good rain. Like domestic cherries, under the flesh there is a thin shell and the meaty inside of the seed.

Uses

The fruit of our wild cherries makes a great trail nibble. I usually see them when they ripen in August and the trail is hot and dry, and the fruit make a refreshing treat. However, don't eat too many of the raw fruit or diarrhea might result.

The wild cherry has a hint of bitterness. The fruit can be cooked off the seeds and the pulp made into jellies, jams, and preserves. You can also make a fruit leather by laying the pulp on a cookie sheet and drying it.

In the old days, the native people enjoyed the flesh of the cherry, but they considered the seed to be the more valuable part of the fruit. The seeds were shelled and the inside meat was cooked and leached to reduce the cyanide. The cooked seeds, once ground into mush or meal, were then used by many native peoples of California to make a sweet bread product or added (like acorns) to stews as a gravy or thickening agent.

Vicki Chiu shows a bowl of cherry seeds, unshelled.

Considering that at least half of the bulk of the collected fruit is the seed, you should at least try processing the seed if you've collected a reasonable volume of the fruit. I wash the seeds, let them dry, and then shell them. We boil through at least 3 changes of water—this takes about 20 minutes—and then we eat the cooked seed as is or grind it to a mush on a metate. Typically, we add the cherry seed mush to acorn flour to make pancakes. The cherry seeds give the acorn pancakes a sweet, almondy flavor.

Caution

If you crush the leaf, it will impart a sweet aroma similar to bitter almond extract used in cooking. That's the telltale aroma of cyanide, so don't use the leaf for tea.

Wild rose shoots

WILD ROSE
Rosa spp.

Use: Fruits eaten raw, cooked, made into jam or tea; wood useful for arrow shafts
Range: Typically riparian but found in many areas; cultivated roses are common in urban areas.
Similarity to toxic species: None
Best time: Fruits mature in summer.
Status: Common
Tools needed: Clippers, possibly gloves

Properties
There are about 100 species of *Rosa* worldwide, which hybridize freely. There are 12 species in California, not including subspecies. Nine of these 12 are natives, including the common *R. californica.*

Wild roses are more common than most people think. They are typically found in wet areas, though this is not a fast rule. The wild rose flowers are 5 petaled, not the multiple-petaled flowers that you find on the hybridized roses. After the flowers mature and fade, the fruit, called the hip, develops; it is usually bright orange and smaller than a grape.

The leaves are oddly divided into 3, 5, or 7 leaflets, and the stalks are covered in thorns. If you've ever had rose bushes in your yard, you have a pretty good idea of what the wild rose looks like.

The wild rose often grows in dense thickets. If it gets cut down, or after a burn, there will be many straight shoots in the new growth.

Rose flower and hip

Uses

For food, we have the flower and the fruits. The flowers have long been used to make rose water and can also be used to make a mild-flavored infusion. The petals make a flavorful, colorful, and nutritious garnish to soups and salads.

Ripe fruit ("hip") of the rose

Wild rose flower RICK ADAMS

The rose hips are one of the richest sources of vitamin C. The fruits can be eaten fresh, but you first should split them open and scrape out the fibrous insides. The fruit is typically a bit fibrous, with a hint of bitterness. More commonly, the fruits can be infused into a tea or made into jellies.

Some old-school archers (such as Alton "Longbow" Safford) consider the rose shaft one of the finest woods to use for making arrows, assuming you cut the new straight shoots. To remove the thorns, you need to then ream the shaft through a rock with a hole in it.

Caution

Before you eat the petals or fruit, make sure the plants have not been sprayed with any pesticides.

Blackberry vine HELEN W.NYERGES

BLACKBERRY
Rubus spp.

Use: Berries used for juices, jams, dessert; dried leaves used for medicine
Range: Riparian and many other areas where sufficient water is supplied
Similarity to toxic species: Somewhat resembles poison oak, though poison oak lacks thorns.
Best time: Fruits mature in the summer.
Status: Common
Tools needed: None, but clippers can help.

Properties
There are about 400–750 species of *Rubus* worldwide. There are 11 in California (not including varieties), and 7 are native. The natives include thimbleberry (*R. parviflorus*). Some are known as raspberries.

Even non-botanists can usually identify the vine and fruit of the very common blackberry. In the northern part of the state and into Oregon, wild blackberries are so common that many just go uneaten.

The leaves are palmately divided (like a hand) into 3, 5, or 7 segments. The vines are twining on the ground or over low hedges and are characterized by their thorns, which make it difficult to wade too deep into any of the old hedge-like stands of wild blackberries.

The white, 5-petaled flowers are followed by the aggregate fruits, which are a collection of sweet drupelets, with the fruit separating from the flower stalk to form a somewhat hollow, thimble-like shape. Most people instantly recognize the shape of the blackberry because they've seen it in the supermarket or in the backyard garden.

Blackberry vine in flower

Uses

A blackberry is easily recognized, and everyone who sees the ripe ones ventures to eat them. I've picked them deep in the chaparral and mountains and along roadsides. The key is to avoid the thorns and to make sure they are not immature and tart. If the fruit is black, soft, and easily picked, it's ripe! You can eat it right away, or pick a bunch and mash them for a topping for pancakes, biscuits, or cake. Even better, add them to vanilla ice cream. (Yes, we know that chocolate ice cream is better for you, but the flavor of blackberries clashes a bit with chocolate.)

You could also make a conserve, a jam, a jelly, a pie filling, or a juice. It's very versatile. And though I rarely have ripe blackberries around long enough to dry them, they can be dried in any food dryer and will keep for quite a while. The dried fruits can then be eaten as is or reconstituted for juices or desserts.

An infusion of the leaves has long been used among Native Americans for diarrhea and childbirth pains.

Fruiting blackberry

JOJOBA FAMILY (SIMMONDSIACEAE)

There is 1 genus to the Jojoba family, and only 1 species to this genus, which is *Simmondsia chinensis*. That means botanists have found this plant to be unique!

Jojoba seed RICK ADAMS

JOJOBA
Simmondsia chinensis

Use: Nuts used for food
Range: Low desert
Similarity to toxic species: None
Best time: Nuts ripen in midsummer.
Status: Somewhat common in its zone
Tools needed: None

Properties
Jojoba (pronounced "hoe-hoe-buh") is an evergreen shrub found throughout the Southwest and into Mexico, especially in arid areas and washes. There is smooth bark and opposite leaves that are leathery, ovate, and dull green. The nutlike fruit is obtusely 3 sided.

Uses
When my friend Nathaniel used to work in the Anza-Borrego area, we'd visit during the summer and pick the fruits off the jojoba bush and eat them. We ate lots of them, and we liked them. We ate them raw; we ate them dried; we ate them roasted.

Jojoba branch with leaves

The jojoba seeds taste a bit better when dried and lightly roasted. We've made many snacks from bowls of these seeds. Yet I hear constantly that you can't eat the seeds "because they make car wax from the seeds." Well, maybe car wax is made from the seeds, but they're certainly edible and tasty.

Like so many conventional or wild foods, everything should always be consumed in moderation until you know how your body reacts to it. Jojoba is no different in this regard. Try a little, see how you like them, and see how your body reacts.

The Cahuilla of the low desert ground the seeds into a powder and made a beverage that was said to be similar to coffee. The Yavapai parched the seeds and ground them into a powder, which had a peanut-butter consistency, and then ate it. Others mashed them into small cakes, which were then boiled and eaten. Though the Indians did eat the fruit, it was not regarded as being highly nutritious because much of the fruit is an indigestible wax.

The oily seeds were also ground into a paste or poultice and applied to sores by the Papago.

Flowering jojoba RICK ADAMS

NIGHTSHADE FAMILY (SOLANACEAE)

There are 75 genera of the Nightshade family and around 3,000 species worldwide. Eleven genera are found in California. Many are toxic, but many are good foods.

Nightshade flower and green fruit

WESTERN NIGHTSHADE, BLACK NIGHTSHADE
Solanum americanum (aka *S. nodiflorum*), *S. douglasii, S. nigrum,* and *S. xanti*

Use: When ripe, fruits are used raw or cooked. Greens are also cooked and eaten.

Range: Disturbed soils, urban areas, chaparral areas

Similarity to toxic species: According to many, this is a toxic species, meaning don't eat the green raw fruits and don't eat the leaves raw. Sickness is likely in either case. There is also a slight resemblance to jimsonweed, which is another plant in the same family and is also toxic.

Best time: Summer

Status: Somewhat common

Tools needed: None

Properties
There are approximately 1,500 species of *Solanum* in the world, with 18 found in California.

Solanum americanum, S. douglasii, and *S. xanti* are natives; *S. nigrum* is not. *S. americanum* and *S. nigrum* are very similar and sometimes difficult to distinguish.

The very young plant resembles lamb's quarter, except that nightshade doesn't have an erect stem; rather, it's more widely branched. Also, though the individual leaves of both nightshade and lamb's quarter are quite similar, nightshade lacks the mealy coating of lamb's quarter as well as the often noticeable red in the axil of the leaf, which is common in lamb's quarter.

Nightshade fruit mostly ripe HELEN W. NYERGES

The 5-petaled white to lavender flower is a very typical nightshade family flower, resembling the flowers of garden tomatoes. The fruits begin as tiny, BB-sized green fruits, and by August they ripen into little purplish-black "tomatoes." We've eaten the ripe fruit from all of the 4 listed *Solanum* species with no problems.

Uses

Fruit

The fruit of this plant seems to peak around August, when the plant can be prolifically in fruit if the season's rain and heat have been just right. Regardless, I have found ripe fruit of the western nightshade during every month of the year in Southern California.

Don't eat these fruits while they are still green, as it could result in a stomachache and minor sickness. That is, you shouldn't eat the green fruits unless they are boiled, fried, or otherwise cooked.

I will try a few of the dark purple ripe fruits when I see them while hiking. I like the fresh tartness. It's very much like eating a tomato but a bit spicier. They are great added to salads—just like adding tomatoes! However, just like tomatoes, there are many other ways to enjoy the western nightshade fruit. We've smashed them and added to pizza dough. They taste like tomatoes, but they turn nearly black when cooked. They are good added to soup, too. Moreover, because they are so small, you don't need to cut or slice; just toss them into your soup or stew.

Also, similar to how sun-dried tomatoes have a unique flavor, you can let western nightshade berries dry in the sun (or in your food dryer) and then eat them as is or reconstitute them later into various recipes. Though it isn't

Green and ripe fruit of nightshade. Note how the flowers nod downward.

absolutely necessary, I find that they dry quicker if you gently smash them first—such as on the cookie sheet where you'll be drying them.

Greens

The young shoots and leaves of these plants are popular in certain cultures around the world. Friends from the Philippines, Mexico, and Hong Kong have told me that the cooked greens are commonly eaten in their homelands. Only the young greens should be used, and they should be at least double-boiled. They are not usually eaten alone, as you might eat spinach, but rather mixed with other vegetables, greens, or meat. In the Philippines, for example, the cooked greens are commonly used in a chicken soup. In Mexico, the nightshade greens are known as *yerba mora*.

Cautions

While there may be other ripe nightshade fruits that could be eaten, we don't advise you eat any but those listed above. Also, do not eat the green berries; only eat the fully ripe, dark purple berries. Otherwise, sickness could result. Green berries should only be consumed if boiled, fried, or otherwise cooked. Anyone with any tomato sensitivity or sensitivity to other members of this family (e.g., eggplant, chiles, peppers) should not consume these fruits.

Do not eat the greens without boiling, changing the water, and boiling again before consuming.

NASTURTIUM FAMILY (TROPAEOLACEAE)

This family has 1 genus and about 90 species worldwide. They are native from Mexico to South America. Its only representative in California is nasturtium.

Nasturtium in flower

NASTURTIUM
Tropaeolum majus

Use: All tender parts can be eaten raw, pickled, or cooked; this includes stems, leaves, flowers, tender seeds.
Range: Originally found along and near the coast; now widely cultivated throughout the urban areas
Similarity to toxic species: None
Best time: Spring
Status: Somewhat common, abundant locally in season

FORAGER NOTE: Though nasturtium is an annual, it is a great choice to grow in a "survival garden" where it can be allowed to reseed itself year after year. This is one of the best plants for the no-work, self-maintaining garden. (Of course, no garden is ever "no-work," but that's another story.)

Properties

Nasturtium plants are found along California's west coast and down into Baja, but they are also commonly found inland as a popular garden plant. Nasturtium seeds are planted in the spring. The seeds are quite interesting because they look like miniature brains: 2-lobed, wrinkled, but green. The plants arise in the spring with the long stems, round in the cross section, and the stem of their round leaves attaching to the bottom of each leaf. The flowers are unique and beautiful, generally coming in shades of brilliant yellow, orange, and red,

Nasturtium flower and leaf

though horticultural varieties have expanded this color spectrum somewhat.

The plant is an annual, and therefore it dies back late every fall. However, if the soil is not disturbed, and there's enough shade and enough moisture, you can guarantee a crop of this beautiful ground cover year after year.

Uses

Everything above ground on the nasturtium is edible. Everything! Just make sure it's still tender and you can eat it: stems, leaves, flowers, seeds. Everything!

Nasturtium leaf

The flowers are probably the most popular because they can be added to salad for a colorful garnish. The leaves are hot, very similar to horseradish, so use them sparingly in your salads. The leaves can be used like grape leaves for dolma, which is typically cooked rice, sometimes with lamb, wrapped in a large leaf.

The stems and leaves are great added to your soups, stews, and egg dishes. They really liven up any dish. You should try adding diced leaves and whole flowers over a rice dish or some freshly cooked MREs (yum!).

The stems alone can be picked, steamed, and served with cheese or butter as a sort of faux green bean, though they are thin. Use only the youngest stems that are tender and snap readily when bent.

I have enjoyed nibbling on the still-green seeds. They are hot and stimulating.

The seeds can also be pickled and made into wild capers. See my recipe below. I had some nasturtium seed pickles that I dated, and the jar was about 20 years old. Believe it or not, they were still very tasty after all that time.

Nasturtium sprawling over a wall

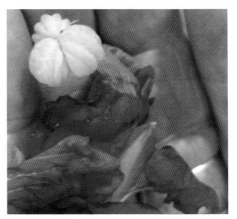

The seed of the nasturtium

RECIPE

Nasturtium "Brain Food" Capers

I keep the pickling process very simple: Just wash the tender, still-green seeds, pack them into a canning jar, and cover with raw apple cider vinegar. Put into your refrigerator for at least 3 weeks before you start serving them. Let your guests know they are "capers."

NETTLE FAMILY (URTICACEAE)

The Nettle family includes 50 genera and 700 species worldwide. Five of those genera are found in California. There are 45 species of *Urtica*, only 2 of which are found in California (not counting 2 subspecies).

Tender leaves at top of nettle plant

STINGING NETTLE
Urtica dioica

Use: Leaves used for food (cooked) and for tea; stalks made into fiber
Range: Riparian, urban fields, edges of farms, disturbed soils, etc.
Similarity to toxic species: None
Best time: Collect the greens in the spring.
Status: Common
Tools needed: Gloves and snippers

FORAGER NOTE: Nettles are an undervalued medicine, and herbalists speak highly of the many uses for nettle tea. I have found that drinking nettle tea in the spring helps to alleviate the symptoms of pollen allergies.

RECIPE

Stinging Nettles Hot Sauce

I created this hot sauce through experimentation and really enjoy it. It has a mild "wild" flavor and is really liked by those who taste it. It's extremely simple to make. This is a very basic recipe, and you can include some of your favorite flavors and ingredients, such as Italian herbs or bay leaves.

Supplies

Latex gloves

Blender (or go primitive with a knife and a *molcajete*)

Jars or bottles

Metal pot

Ingredients

5 ounces jalapeño chiles, stemmed and chopped with seeds (make sure they're not too hot, though)

1 ounce serrano chiles

5 ounces fresh nettle leaves (or young nettles)

Juice from 2 limes

6 garlic cloves

3½ cups raw apple cider vinegar

1 teaspoon kosher or pickling salt

1 cup water or white wine (I used white wine in my original recipe.)

Combine all the ingredients, and blend until smooth. Strain for a thinner sauce, or keep it as is. Transfer to jars and cover. Refrigerate for at least 2 weeks and then enjoy.

—RECIPE FROM PASCAL BAUDAR

Properties

This perennial generally sends up a single stalk in the winter or spring that can reach around 5' tall if undisturbed. The leaves are oblong with toothed margins and taper to a point. Both the leaves and stalks are covered with needles or bristles that cause a stinging irritation when you brush against them.

Though it's a European native, you can find it all over California, along streams in the wilderness, and in fields and backyards.

Uses

The young, tender leaf tips of nettle are the best to use, though you could also collect just the leaves later in the season (the stems get too tough). These tender tops can be steamed and boiled, which removes the stingy-ness of nettles. They are tasty as a spinach dish, alone or served with butter, cheese, or other topping. Also try the water from the boiling—it's delicious!

We've also made tasty stews and soups, which we began by boiling the nettle tops. Then we quickly added diced potatoes, some red onions, and other greens. Often miso powder was added, or not. Cook until tender and serve, or add Braggs Liquid Amino Acid for some great flavor and nutrition.

This is a vitamin-rich plant, so you'll be getting your medicine when you eat it.

Nettle leaves

Because the nettle plant is only available seasonally in the spring, I harvest as much as I am able each year. I freeze some to use in soups, and I dry as much as I'm able. If I am using the dried leaves for tea, I simply take a small amount of the entire dried plant for each pot of tea, stems and all. If I am making soup, I remove all stems and sift the leaves to get a fine powder, which I typically make into a miso soup.

We also take the sifted nettle powder and mix it 50-50 with flour to make a pancake batter. These make excellent pancakes (you could also make bread or biscuits), either eaten plain or with some topping like jam.

Medicinal

When I have severe allergies in the spring from various pollens, an infusion of dried nettles is one of my best remedies. However, despite all the medicinal uses for nettles listed in herbal literature, I've not found any data to support why nettle tea is helpful for me in this manner. Nettle leaf tea is widely regarded as an astringent, diuretic, and useful in cases of excessive menstruation. Herbalist Michael Moore states that the nettle seeds are an excellent lung astringent, particularly useful after bronchitis to help return tone and capillary strength to the bronchial mucosa. When I dry nettles for tea, I dry the entire herb and remove the stems when fully dry. Thus, my tea generally has seed mixed with the leaf.

Cordage

The mature nettle stalks have long been used as a source of fiber to make cordage, which has been used for bowstrings and other utilitarian purposes. The stalks can be processed in a number of ways, such as first soaking in water to soften and then gently beating with a piece of wood to express only the fiber.

Nettle dries in this open-air mesh drying rack.

Cautions

As you will probably learn from personal experience, you get "stung" when you brush up against nettle. This is due to the formic acid within each "needle" or "bristle," which causes skin irritation. Be careful when you gather nettle greens, and be sure to wear gloves or other protection. And if you do get the nettle rash, you can treat it with fresh aloe vera gel, or with the freshly crushed leaves of other plants such as chickweed or curly dock.

GRAPE FAMILY (VITACEAE)

The Grape family has about 15 genera and about 800 species worldwide. In California, it is represented by only 2 genera, *Parthenocissus* (the Virginia creeper) and *Vitis* (grapes).

Wild grape vines HELEN W. NYERGES

WILD GRAPE
Vitis spp.

Use: Fruits eaten raw or cooked; leaves used in Middle Eastern cooking
Range: Prefers riparian areas and moist, shady canyons
Similarity to toxic species: Wild cucumber (*Marah* spp.) could be confused with wild grapes when young. However, once they begin to fruit, wild cucumber fruits (which are large and oval-shaped, about 4" long) bear no resemblance to grapes.
Best time: The fruits mature in the summer; leaves are best collected in spring.
Status: Widespread
Tools needed: None, but clippers can be useful.

Properties
Though there are 65 known species of *Vitis*, it is only represented in California by 3 species, 1 of which (*V. vinifera*) is the introduced cultivated grape. The other

2 are the California wild grape (*V. californica*) and the desert wild grape (*V. girdiana*).

Anyone who has ever grown grapes or visited a vineyard can automatically recognize our 2 wild grapes. Typically growing along streams or in moist canyons, these are sprawling vining plants that often cover entire hillsides and whatever vegetation is growing there.

You can usually see peeling bark on the woody stems and tendrils opposite each leaf. The bottom of the young leaf is tomentose (covered with fine hairs), less so as the leaf matures. The fruit clusters tend to be more sparse than cultivated grapes, and sometimes (depending on the location and the season) there is a lot of leaf and vine and very little fruit.

Flowering wild grape

Uses

I first learned about our native grape when reading the accounts of the first Spanish explorers to come into Southern California's Native American territory. They wrote that the California natives were eating acorns, wild grasses, and wild grapes. The more I observed, the more I realized that our wild grape was very widespread.

My first use of this plant was when my friend Talal was getting married. He's from Lebanon, and he wanted to make some Middle Eastern grape leaves for the wedding reception. We went up into the local mountains and collected

Wild grape with green fruit

many of the youngest wild grape leaves. We then boiled them to soften, added a tablespoon of cooked rice on each leaf, and then rolled it. We put about two dozen of these in a pan and cooked them further. They were delicious!

However, mostly people think of the fruit when considering grapes. Commercial grapevines are far better producers of the fruit because growers prune the vines back so they get more sun and they fertilize them. Wild grapes produce endlessly long vines and often just a few fruits per cluster. In a dry year, you may not find any grapes at all. But if you do and your timing is right, you can create some wonderful dishes from the wild grapes. On a few occasions, I've had wild grapes that could be eaten out of hand

Wild grape vines sprawling over hillside

similar to table grapes, but that is the exception. Generally, wild grapes are very tart and must be cooked. Once cooked, however, you can make some delicious juices, jams, jellies, and sauces, or even just dry them for wild raisins.

Sometimes the desert natives made a cooked mush from grapes.

Grape leaves have sometimes been made into a poultice for wounds.

The vines can also be used for weaving baskets and for other uses where the fiber will not be under tension.

Monocots

These plants have one cotyledon. Leaf veins are generally parallel from the base or midrib, and flower parts are generally in threes. Some examples of monocots include all grasses, cattails, rushes, palms, all lilies, and all onion family members.

CENTURY PLANT FAMILY (AGAVACEAE)

There are 23 genera and 637 species worldwide in this family. Eight of those genera are found in California.

Christopher next to flowering yucca RICK ADAMS

YUCCA
*Hesperoyucca whipplei (*formerly *Yucca whipplei)*

Use: Immature flower stalk, flowers, fruits, and seeds can be used for food; the leaves are an excellent fiber and soap source.
Range: This yucca is found mostly in the desert and chaparral regions of the southern part of the state.
Similarity to toxic species: None
Best time: The food sources are available from mid-spring to about midsummer; leaves can be gathered at any time.
Status: Relatively common
Tools needed: Clippers (I always use Florian ratchet clippers) for the leaf; sharp knife for other parts

FORAGER NOTE: The leaves (used green, or dried but moistened before using) are excellent for making twine, braids, sandals, hats, nets, net bags, or any item requiring twine or rope. The green leaves, when shredded and agitated with water, produce a quality soap for washing skin, clothing, dogs, and so on. The dried flower stalks can be hollowed and used for quivers, drums, or general-purpose carrying cases.

Properties

Though there are 3 species of *Hesperoyucca,* there is only *H. whipplei* in California. This very common yucca had formerly been classified as part of the *Yucca* genus, which includes banana yucca (*Y. baccata*), Joshua tree (*Y. brevifolia*), and Mojave yucca (*Y. schidigera*).

Yuccas are a somewhat ubiquitous plant in many locales, including the deserts, the chaparral, and the lower elevations of the mountains. The leaves are long, lance shaped, and very fibrous with a sharp tip. Some varieties have sharp edges.

The white to cream-colored flowers are produced when the plant is in its final season.

Yucca looks similar to a giant pincushion of leaves that are up to 2' long and 1"–2" wide.

The plants will grow for 20 years or more, then flower one spring and die that season. The beginning of the flower stalk appears similar to a huge asparagus, somewhat red in color. As this flower stalk grows taller in April or May, it begins to flower with its clusters of creamy-white flowers. There are 6 perianth segments (sepals and petals) of the flowers. By summer, the green fruits develop. The fruits are capsules that have a few chambers. When the fruits mature, the flat black seeds will develop in these chambers, stacked like sliced bread.

Yucca plant in the forest

Pickled Yucca Shoots

I've pickled *H. whipplei* shoots for several years now, and they've even been served in some of the top restaurants in Los Angeles. The recipe is very simple.

For this recipe, we use half-pint jars.

Peel and slice the fresh yucca shoot into small ½" squares. Fill up the jar with as many squares as you can, and in each jar, place the following:

1 garlic clove

¼ California bay leaf (or ⅓ regular bay leaf)

1 small- to medium-size spicy dehydrated chile (just because I like some heat)

1 teaspoon grated ginger or a nice chunk of ginger (around ½" cube)

Make a pickling solution of 2 cups raw apple cider vinegar, 2 cups white wine (or water), ½ cup sugar, and 2 teaspoons sea salt. Depending on how many jars you're making, you may need to make more. Bring the solution to a boil and pour it into the jars, covering the yucca.

Close the lids and place the jars in the fridge. Wait 2–3 weeks before consuming.

If you know how to can and want to preserve them outside the fridge (shelf-stable), use the water-bath method and boil for 15 minutes.

—RECIPE FROM PASCAL BAUDAR

Uses

Though yucca was probably one of the most important fiber plants of the Southern California Native Americans, let's first look at the food uses.

In the spring, when you find a yucca plant that is beginning its flowering death dance, it will begin by sending up its asparagus-like immature stalk that can be cut, peeled, and eaten raw, though it's better boiled, sautéed, or cooked into a mixed vegetable dish.

Next, assuming you didn't cut down the stalk, the plant begins to flower with these beautiful creamy-white flowers. The flowers have traditionally been eaten in a number of ways; perhaps the most common is to first boil them (to remove the soapiness), drain, add flour, form into patties, and then sauté. They could also simply be boiled and seasoned.

The fruits that follow are also good, and you need to get them while they are still white inside. They are probably best baked in your oven or in the coals at the edge of the campfire. They are reminiscent of cooked squash.

Lastly, the flat black seeds could be collected once the fruits mature in mid- to late summer. The seeds are best ground into a flour and used with other flours to produce various pastry products such as biscuits or pancakes. (However, I have yet to meet anyone who actually likes the flavor of the yucca seeds.)

In Mexico, the flowers of some species of yucca are boiled, then mixed with flour and spices, and shaped into patties and cooked. It's like eating a vegetarian burger.

Yucca plant sending up its flower stalk
HELEN W. NYERGES

Brush on right made from roots and wire, from a Mexican market. All other brushes made from yucca leaf, in traditional style.

Dried yucca flowering stalk has been hollowed out and used for "hot-rock" cooking.

Four-leaf Mogollon-style yucca sandal, tried on by Paul Campbell

ONION OR GARLIC FAMILY (ALLIACEAE)

There are 13 genera and 750–800 species of the Onion family worldwide. Three genera are found in California, with *Allium* being by far the largest.

Wild onion flower

WILD ONIONS et al.
Allium spp.

Use: Bulbs and greens eaten raw or cooked. However, I strongly advise readers to leave the bulbs in the ground and only pick the greens for food.

Range: The habitat of the 52 species of wild onions found in California represents collectively just about every type of environment.

Similarity to toxic species: Wild onions were once categorized in the Lily family because these 2 groups are so similar, and the flowers of most are nearly identical. There are deadly members of the Lily family, so never eat any member of this group unless you are absolutely certain you have made positive identification.

Best time: The leaves and flowers are most noticeable in the spring and early summer.

Status: Though in certain areas you will not find wild onions, they can be common locally.

Tools needed: None

Properties

In California, 52 species (not including varieties) of *Allium* can be found. Most are natives.

Wild onions go by many names: ramps, wild garlic, leek, to name a few.

In general, wild onions look like small green onions from the market, though many are inconspicuous when not in flower. There is a small underground bulb, and the leaves are green and hollow. The flower stalk tends to be a bit more fibrous than the leaves. There appears to be 6 petals of the same color; in fact, there are 3 sepals underneath the 3 identical petals, giving the appearance of a 6-petaled flower. The expedient field key to identifying a wild onion is the unmistakable aroma. If you don't have that aroma, you shouldn't use the plant, because similar-appearing members of the Lily family could be poisonous.

Wild onions actually can be found all over the United States

Wild onion plant in flower HELEN W. NYERGES

in a broad diversity of ecotypes. Here in California, we find a lot in the desert regions and in higher-elevation meadows and fields. We notice them mostly when they flower, because otherwise they appear very similar to grass.

Uses

When you find wild onions, you'll be tempted to pull up the plant so you can eat the bulb. That's what you do in your own garden, but that's not the only way you can use these. Generally, I only pick the green leaves for consumption. If there are a lot of the wild onions, I might take some of the bulbs to eat, break up the cluster, and replant some. The reason that I generally only eat the greens is that I've seen some patches of wild onions disappear entirely due to foragers uprooting the whole plant.

I used to hike with a man who always uprooted the wild onions to eat in his sandwiches and other dishes. One time, as we walked by what had been his favorite patch, he noted aloud that there were not many wild onions there anymore. Guess what? He had picked them! Two years later, he noted with dismay that there were no more wild onions at the particular spot by the river where we hiked. "Don't you know why?" I asked him. "You picked them all! You picked the roots. How did you expect them to perpetuate?" "Oh?" he responded. "Really?"

While the wild onion bulbs can be used in any of the myriad ways in which you're used to eating garlic, onions, chives, leeks, and so on, you'll still get most of the flavor and most of the nutritional benefits by eating only the leaves.

I pinch off a few leaves here, a few there, and I add them to salads. Diced, they're great in soups, stews, egg dishes, and stir-fries. Also, if you ever have to live off MREs, you'd spice them up and add to their nutritional value by adding any of the wild onion greens.

All tender parts of wild onions are edible, above- and belowground. Generally, the older flower stalks become fibrous and unpalatable.

Wild onion showing roots RICK ADAMS

Otherwise, the bulbs and leaves are all used raw or cooked. Simply remove any outer fibrous layers of the plant, rinse, and then use in any of the ways you'd use green onions or chives.

Wild onions can be added to salads, used as the base for a soup, cooked alone similar to spinach, chopped and mixed into eggs, cooked as a side to fish, and used to enhance countless other recipes. Wild onions share many of the healthful benefits of garlic and improve any urban or wilderness meal. Backpackers who are relying on dried trail rations will certainly enjoy the sustenance of the wild onions.

Many Native Americans heavily relied on wild onions and regarded them as staples, not just condiments.

There are excellent health benefits associated with eating any members of this group. Some of these benefits include lowering of cholesterol levels, flu prevention, and reduction of high blood pressure. Used externally, the crushed green leaves can be applied directly to wounds to prevent infection.

Cautions

Never forget that some members of the Lily family with bulbs are deadly poisonous if eaten. Wild onions used to be classified within the Lily family because their characteristics are so similar. Therefore, make absolutely certain that you have correctly identified any wild onions that you intend to eat. You should check the floral characteristics to be certain that there are 3 sepals and 3 petals. Then make sure you detect an obvious onion aroma; if there is none, do not eat the plant. Though there are a few true onions that lack the onion aroma, it is imperative that you have absolutely identified those nonaromatic species as safe before you prepare them in your lunch.

PALM FAMILY (ARECACEAE)

Worldwide, there are about 200 genera and about 3,000 species in the Palm family. These are very conspicuous trees throughout California, widely planted as a street and park tree. Typically, there is the large trunk, which could be fat or somewhat skinny, and can rise about 65' (in the case of our only native, the California fan palm) or as tall as a five-story building (in the case of the Canary Island date palm, which is not native but has widely naturalized in our state). There is typically the trunk with the fronds arising from the crown. The fronds are either palmately or pinnately lobed. The palmate leaves are formed on a stem; these are the fan palms. The leaves can also form as pinnately lobed leaves, or feather fronds. The fruits are usually drupes and are generally called dates. There is the common date palm with the sweet fruits and 2-lobed seed, and there are also the little black, round-to-ovate fruits from the native palm.

California has 2 genera of the Palm family.

Cluster of immature palm fruits (dates)

CALIFORNIA FAN PALM
Washingtonia filifera

Use: Fruits are edible fresh or dried. Dried fruit (minus the seed) is used in many dishes. Leaves are used in many utilities, such as fire making, shelter, etc.

Range: California fan palm is restricted in the wild to the low desert, but cultivated palms are found everywhere.

Similarity to toxic species: None

Best time: Fruits in the summer

Status: Scattered, common locally

Tools needed: Usually you pick the fruit off the ground. If you can't wait, you'll need a ladder.

Properties

There are only 2 species of *Washingtonia*, and *W. filifera* is the native species. The other is the Mexican fan palm (*W. robusta*), native to Baja California.

Though not widespread, the California fan palm is very common in certain locales, such as Palm Springs. The main trunk arises 60'–65', and the dried fronds are often seen hanging down the stalk. The leaves are similar to fans, with the outstretched leaflets arising from a common stem. The fruits are small and black.

Native palms in Palm Canyon, Cahuilla territory near Palm Springs RICK ADAMS

Traditional shelter made from palm fronds RICK ADAMS

Uses

The little fruits can be collected and eaten as is, spitting out the seed. The local Indians ground the fruits, sometimes seed and all, into a sweet flour that was then used for a sweet gravy or a drink. The powder can be added to other foods as a sweetener, just as you'd add white sugar in a modern diet.

Note: Because various parts of palms can be used in the same way, the following comments can be applied somewhat generically to all of the palms and don't necessarily apply exclusively to the California fan palm.

When the tree is cut down, the inside heart can be cut out and eaten. Yes, you will need saws and/or

Tree-pruner shows recently cut heart from a palm tree.

Alan Halcon shows a cluster of the mature California fan palm seed.

machetes to do this effectively. The white, edible part is at the base of the leaves, in the very middle of the plant. If it is not very tender, it won't be good to eat. The hearts can be eaten raw, boiled, or stir-fried, and they can be pickled as well. It's a delicious food from the palm tree.

The dried leaves of most palms have multiple craft uses. They are good for making baskets, hats, sandals, and other woven goods. They can be used as the thatching for homes as they were by the desert Native Americans in days gone by.

The stem of the fan palm is of the ideal balance between softness and hardness for a hearth for making fire with a hand drill or bow drill.

SPIDERWORT FAMILY (COMMELINACEAE)

This family contains about 40 genera and 630 species worldwide, mostly found in the tropics, with some (commonly called "wandering Jews") cultivated as ornamentals.

In California, we have only 2 genera commonly found in the wild: *Tradescantia* and *Commelina*; only 1 species of each is represented. Though we are presenting information about each plant individually, the plants are commonly mistaken for one another because when not in flower, they are very similar. Also, because they are both used in the same fashion, the information in the Uses section is the same for each. Both plants will grow readily from vegetative cuttings.

WANDERING JEW
Tradescantia fluminensis

Use: Entire aboveground plant used raw or cooked
Range: Urban yards, riparian areas near urban areas, open fields with shade, etc.; can be invasive

Wandering Jew

Similarity to toxic species: None
Best time: Can be harvested year-round
Status: Common in certain areas
Tools needed: None

Properties

This is a trailing, ground-cover plant with succulent stems and leaves that are alternately arranged on the stem. The parallel-veined leaves are forest green, with a sheath at the base of the leaf that clasps the stem and comes to a sharp point. Sometimes they are streaked with lighter green stripes.

The little white, 3-petaled flowers appear in clusters at the stem tips from spring through fall.

This is native to Brazil and Argentina, where it is regarded as an agricultural pest. It creates quick ground cover in urban areas and generally takes care of itself with no help from the homeowner. It has also been spotted sprawling in mountain areas, typically where there was once a cabin where ornamentals were planted.

Uses

Same as for tropical spiderwort (see next entry).

Tropical spiderwort

TROPICAL SPIDERWORT
Commelina benghalensis

Use: Entire aboveground plant used raw or cooked
Range: Urban yards, riparian areas near urban areas, open fields with shade, etc.; can be invasive
Similarity to toxic species: None
Best time: Can be harvested year-round
Status: Common in certain areas
Tools needed: None

Properties
Tropical spiderwort is very similar to wandering Jew, though the leaf edges are often wavy or wrinkly. The flower is blue, and though there are 3 parts, 2 are larger and showy.

Uses
Because this plant is so common, I was happy to learn that I could use it in various dishes. My first awareness of its use as food came from a Filipino friend who told me that he ate it in a stew back home. Cooked alone (similar to spinach), spiderwort leaves and tender stems are bland, but otherwise they make

Tropical spiderwort in flower

a good cooked green. I have added the leaves in moderate amounts to stews, soups, mixed sautéed dishes, and egg dishes. Because the leaves are not strongly flavored, they go well with most dishes. Blending it with other more strongly flavored wild leaves makes a tastier dish.

The tender parts of this plant can also be added to most cooked dishes, such as stews and soups. Make a broth (miso, chicken broth, whatever) and add maybe a half cup of the leaves along with a half cup of other wild greens; a blend is always better. You can also just cook up the greens, drain, and serve seasoned with butter or cheese.

I have had salads that were primarily spiderwort (either one of the two described), which we rinsed and diced, and added avocado and dressing. This makes a good salad, but again, you get a better salad by adding a variety of greens.

I have a wild-food friend who likes to make many variations of kimchee. One variation includes a lot of the green spiderwort leaves, stems, and flower buds. The vinegar makes this a tasty treat. My friend has also used the purple wandering Jew flowers and tender stems in his wild kimchee, and though he says it's OK, it's not my favorite dish.

The only downside we've noted is that when consuming good portions of these greens, loose bowels can result.

The tropical spiderwort is used medicinally in China and to feed animals in Pakistan, Africa, and Southeast Asia. It is eaten by people in Pakistan and Nepal, and it is regarded as "famine" food in India.

RUSH FAMILY (JUNCACEAE)

The Rush family has 7 genera and 440 species worldwide. In California, it is represented by only 2 genera.

Leaves and seeds of rush

RUSH
Juncus textilis et al.

Use: Tender white growth at base of shoots edible raw or cooked; seeds cooked in pastry or porridge
Range: Riparian areas
Similarity to toxic species: None
Best time: Spring for the shoots; fall for the seed
Status: Common locally
Tools needed: None

Properties
There are 315 species of *Juncus* worldwide. In California, there are 64 species (not counting varieties), and all but 8 are native.

When seeing *Juncus* for the first time, many folks will think it's a type of grass, cattail, or perhaps reed. Yes, it has a grasslike appearance, but there are some important differences that put this plant into a different family.

The leaves are long, grasslike, and hollow from top to bottom. There are various lengths of *Juncus,* and *J. textilis* can be found in thick patches 5'–6' tall. The leaves are round in the cross section. The flowers are inconspicuous bits of seed on the end of long stems, tassel-like, and are formed near the top of each leaf, generally off to one side.

Like many grasses and cattails, these spread with an underground system of rhizomes.

They are typically found in association with wet areas, such as a spring or river, though they are not necessarily right in the water, such as you'd find with watercress.

Uses

This plant and its close relatives are regarded as some of the best weaving materials for baskets, mats, and other woven products. In addition, there are at least two good food sources from this plant as well.

In the fall, there will be a small tassel of seeds on the top portion of the rushes. If you're there at the right time, you can put a bag under the tassel and shake out the seed. These seeds are then used in the two ways in which most grains can be used: mixed in with pastry products or as a cooked cereal.

In the spring, you can gently pull up the long leaves and note that the bottom of the plant is white and tender. There's not a lot of food here, but it's good, and you can get a lot in a short period of time. You can eat them raw on the spot, or save them to add to salads, stir-fries, or soups.

Harvesting the shoots seems to make the rush patches grow better, but you still shouldn't just pick these for the tender base and then discard the rest, because you really only get a nibble from each shoot. The upper part of the plant—the long leaves—are great for making traditional baskets. If you're going to eat some of the young bases, you should really collect the shoots and use them for weaving, or give them to someone who makes baskets. Unless, of course, you're lost and starving, which is a wholly different situation.

FORAGER NOTE: Properly prepared, these leaves are ideal for many of the traditional basketry done by California Native Americans. One of the best how-to descriptions of this is found in Paul Campbell's *Survival Skills of Native California.*

GRASS FAMILY (POACEAE)

This family was formerly called Gramineae. Worldwide, there are 650–900 genera with about 10,550 species. There are so many species that the family is divided into 5 major categories. In California, there are 115 genera and hundreds of species.

The Grass family has the "greatest economic importance of any family," according to botanist Mary Barkworth, citing wheat, rice, maize, millet, sorghum, sugarcane, forage crops, weeds, thatching, weaving, and building materials.

Indian rice grass in seed

Use: Leaves for food (sprouts, juiced, etc.); seeds for flour or meal

Range: Grasses are truly found everywhere.

Similarity to toxic species: None

Best time: Somewhat varies depending on what grass we're talking about but generally spring for the greens and summer to fall for seed

Status: Very common

Tools needed: None

Properties

The large plant family Poaceae (or Gramineae) is characterized by mostly herbaceous but sometimes woody plants with hollow and jointed stems; narrow, alternate sheathing leaves; petalless flowers borne in spikelets; and fruit in the form of seedlike grain. Ranging in size from little annuals to giant bamboos, the family includes bamboo; sugarcane; numerous grasses; and cereal grains such as barley, corn, oats, rice, rye, and wheat.

Wild oats in front of a sycamore tree

The flowering and seed structures are rather diverse, ranging from the stickery seeds of the foxtail grasses that get caught in your socks to the open clusters of sorghum, such seeds as rice and wheat, and the kernels of corn. Indeed, whole books have been written describing the diversity of this large family.

Uses

The edibility of the wild grasses, generically, can be summed up in two categories: the young leaves and the seeds.

You may have had some of the leaf when you went to a health-food store and ordered wheatgrass juice. That's perhaps one of the best ways to eat various grass leaves—juice them. You can purchase an electric or a hand-crank juicer. I have juiced various wild-grass leaves and found the flavors to be quite diverse. Some have the flavor of wheatgrass juice and are good added to drinks or to soup broth. Some are very different, almost like seaweed, and these are typically better in soup. However you do it, get the grasses as young as possible. They are most nutritious at this stage, and they are less fibrous. You will discover that grasses contain a *lot* of fiber once you start to crank a hand juicer, watching the green liquid gold come out one end and the strands of fiber come out the other end.

If you don't have a juicer, you could eat the very young grass leaves in salads or soups, though you may find yourself chewing and chewing and, ultimately, spitting out fiber.

The seeds of all grasses are theoretically edible, though harvesting them is very difficult—if not next to impossible—in some cases. Some grass seeds are easy to collect by hand. They are then winnowed. Some are very easy to winnow off the outer chaff; some are more problematic. I have taken some of the foxtail grass seeds, put them in a small metal strainer, and passed them through a fire to burn off the outer covering. Though I was left with a little seed, I found this method less fruitful than simply locating other grasses with more readily harvestable seeds.

The seeds you gather for food should be mature and have no foreign growths on them. Then you either grind them into flour for pastry products (bread, biscuits, etc.), or you cook them into mush (like a cereal mush).

With thousands of species worldwide on every landmass, and large numbers found in California, the grasses are a group that we should get to know better. Not only are they arguably more important than trees in holding the earth together—their combined root systems are vast—but they are a valuable food source, assuming you are there at the right time to harvest the seed or leaf.

CATTAIL FAMILY (TYPHACEAE)
The Cattail family contains 2 genera and about 32 species worldwide.

Mature brown cattail spike

CATTAIL
Typha spp.

Use: Food (inner rhizome, young white shoots, green female spike, yellow male pollen); leaves excellent for fiber crafts where high tensile strength is not required
Range: Wetlands
Similarity to toxic species: None
Best time: Generally, the shoots and spikes are best collected in the spring. The rhizome could be collected at any time.
Status: Common in wetlands
Tools needed: Clippers, possibly a trowel

Properties

The *Typha* genus contains about 15 species worldwide, with 3 of those species in California. Each of those 3 is considered native.

Everyone everywhere knows cattail—think of it as that grassy plant in the swamps that looks similar to a hot dog on a stick. Always growing in slow-moving waters or the edges of streams, cattail has long flat leaves that grow 6' long and taller, arising from the underground horizontal rhizomes. When the plants flower in spring, the flower spike is green with yellowish pollen at the top. As it matures, the green spike ripens to a brown color, creating the familiar fall decoration—the hot dog on the stick.

Uses

Euell Gibbons, author of *Stalking the Wild Asparagus* and many other wild-food books, used to refer to cattails as the "supermar-

Green cattail spike RICK ADAMS

ket of the swamps," which is a good description of this versatile plant.

There are at least four good food sources from the cattail, which I'll list in order of my preference.

In the spring, the plant sends up its green shoots. If you get to them before they stiffen and the flower spike has started, you can tug them up, and the shoot breaks off from the rhizome. You then cut the lower foot or so and peel off the green layers. The inner white layer is eaten raw or cooked. It looks like a green onion, but the flavor is similar to cucumber.

The spike is the lower part of the flower spike and is technically the female part of the flower. You find the spike in spring when it's entirely green and tender. Though you could eat it raw, it's far better boiled. Cook it, butter it, and eat it like corn on the cob. Guess what? It even tastes like corn on the cob. You could also scrape off the green edible portion from the woody core and add to

David Martinez checks out the mature brown cattail spike.

stews or stir-fries, or even shape into patties (with egg or flour added) and cook similar to burgers.

The pollen is the fine yellow material that you can shake out of the flower spikes. The flower spike is divided into 2 sections—the lower female part, described above, and directly on top, the less-substantial male section, which produces the fine yellow pollen. If you're in the swamp at the right time, typically April or May, you can shake lots of pollen into a bag, strain it (to remove twigs and bugs), and use it in any pastry product.

The rhizome is also a good starchy food. Pull out the long horizontal roots from the mud, wash them, and then peel off the soft outer layer. You could just chew on the inner part of the rhizome if you need the energy from the natural sugar, or you could process it a bit. One method of processing involves mashing or grinding up the inner rhizome and then putting it into a jar of water. As the water settles, the pure starch will be on the bottom and the fiber will be floating on the top, so you can easily scoop it out and discard it. The starch is then used in soups or in pastry and bread products.

Angelo Cervera shows the ready-to-cook green cattail spikes.

Aside from cooking, the long green leaves have a lengthy history of being made into various woven products that will not be used under tension, such as baskets, sandals, hats, and even for the outer layers of the homes utilized by many of the natives of old California.

Moreover, when that cattail spike matures to a chocolate-brown color, break it open, and it all turns to an insulating fluff. Each tiny seed is actually connected to a bit of fluff that aids in the transportation of that seed to greener grass on the other side. You can use that fluff to stop the bleeding of a minor wound, as an alternative to down when stuffing a sleeping bag or coat, and as a fantastic fire starter!

OTHER EDIBLES

Do you have a favorite California wild food that isn't listed here? Remember, it was our intent to include those California plants that are the most widespread, readily recognizable, and those that would make a significant contribution to your meals. We also wanted to have plants that represented most of the biological zones in our state. However, as you continue your study of ethnobotany, you will discover that there are many more wild plants that could be used for food. Some are marginal, and some just aren't that great.

I have eaten California ragweed, various species of *Phacelia* and *Bidens,* telegraph weed, and many others that I never found described in a wild-food or ethnobotany book. Yes, they are edible, but after trying them, I realized why ancient people never used them, or only used them when nothing else was available.

Yes, there are many wild animals and ocean life in California that could be used for food. We have deliberately chosen to stick to the plants.

Mycology

If you want to begin using wild mushrooms for food, I am of the opinion that you should plan on spending as much time as you devote to at least a four-unit college course for at least two semesters, preferably more.

There are many reasons for this. For the most part, you cannot go back day after day to the same mushroom to study it in detail and watch its growth cycle. Mushrooms come suddenly and decompose just as rapidly. They are not like the oak tree that will be there every day.

While you should be able to identify a dozen or so common edible mushrooms after some initial study, keep in mind that not all mushrooms have been identified, and even less is known about the edibility of most species.

Yucca plant HELEN W. NYERGES

Moreover, in their attempt to further clarify the relationships of mushrooms, mycologists occasionally rename a mushroom. The changes in Latin names causes initial confusion to wild-food foragers. Also, don't forget that the mushroom you just found may not be in your book or database. Don't assume that the mushroom in your hand or in the ground in front of you must be in your book. When in doubt, do without!

Also, though I regularly eat about two dozen wild mushrooms, I am always humbled by the occasional newspaper article describing how a lifelong mycologist ate the wrong mushroom and died!

There are many books and videos today that are exclusively devoted to giving you an understanding of how mushrooms grow, their classification, and how to accurately identify those that are edible. Even better than books and videos are classes and clubs where you go into the field and see the mushrooms for yourself.

GETTING STARTED

Exploring the Fascinating World of Wild Plants

During the many field trips and classes that I have conducted since 1974, I have often been asked how I got interested in the subject of edible wild plants.

Where I grew up in Pasadena, we were close to the San Gabriel Mountain range and the Angeles National Forest to the north. Going to the mountains was often an after-school or weekend recreation choice. During grammar school, we went to the mountains just to hike and explore and perhaps to run on the trails. Eventually, my brother and various friends would go out on backpacking trips, carrying heavy loads—the bulk of the weight was typically canned goods. The most unpleasant aspect of those trips was carrying all that weight. But back then, I was not aware of alternatives. Gradually, I learned that there was a lot you didn't need to bring, and I learned that you could carry dried goods from the supermarket that cost a lot less than the freeze-dried food at the backpacking shops. That helped a little bit.

One day, probably in 1969 or 1970, I was resting with a friend at a place called Inspiration Point where there was a terrific view of the Los Angeles basin to the south. Another hiker came by, and we got to talking about backpacking things and about Native American skills. As we talked, the man told us that he'd studied with some natives in Northern California who'd taught him some of the wild-food plants that people ate in the "old days." He said that most of those plants are still with us. We looked around at our high-elevation locale, and he pointed to the mustard plants and the pine trees as two examples of foods. Though those examples didn't seem all that appealing, something clicked inside my mind. That's it, I thought. I'd like to learn how to do that. I'd be able to survive wilderness situations, and I could carry less weight in my pack. The man was just there for a few minutes, and then he hiked on, but I thought about it all day. Gradually, I began buying books, checking out library books, taking botany classes, going on field trips, and getting to know anyone who knew anything about the usefulness of plants.

Another factor stimulated my interest. In the mid-1970s, there were many businesses selling boxes of dehydrated food, wheat, and other necessities so families could survive the "major famine that is sure to hit the United States around 1978." Well, the famine didn't happen, but the fear factor stimulated me to research agriculture and what we do to the land to raise food, how we store and transport food, and all the hundreds of intricate steps that make up what we call the "food distribution system." Frankly, back then in my teens, this eye-opening research shocked and frightened me, and I was convinced that all I needed to do to personally survive was to learn about wild edible plants.

These, and other factors, led me on the path of mycology, botany, ethnobotany, and taxonomy. It is a path I have never left.

In January of 1974, I began to lead wild-food outings that were organized by WTI (White Tower Inc.), a nonprofit organization focused entirely on education in all aspects of survival. I led half-day walks where we'd go into a small area, identify and collect plants, and make a salad and maybe soup and tea on the spot. I became an active member of the Los Angeles Mycological Association and made rapid progress in learning about how to identify and use mushrooms. Also, I continued to take specialized classes and field trips in botany, biology, taxonomy, and ethnobotany. I spent many hours in the classroom of Dr. Leonid Enari, who was the chief botanist at the Los Angeles County Arboretum in Arcadia. He was a walking encyclopedia, and he also took the time to mentor me, to answer all my plant questions, and to help me with my first wild-food book.

Though I have spent long hours studying books, my quick and primary source of learning has always been direct field experience with an expert, such as Dr. Enari and others. I have been humbled many times, thinking that I knew "a lot," only to go to a nearby field or mountainside filled with flora that appeared totally unfamiliar to me. Gradually, little by little, I came to know the plants of the fields, the chaparral, the mountains, the ocean areas, and the deserts.

Let's review the learning process:

- Don't worry about trying to know everything at once. That idea just clutters up your mind. Find a skilled naturalist or botanist to go on a walk with you in your own backyard or neighborhood, somewhere close to where you live. Take lots of notes and photos for your review, but get out into the field with a knowledgeable person.
- Regularly review the plants you saw during your neighborhood walk. Observe their changes throughout the seasons so you know what they look like as a sprout, as an adolescent, as a mature and flowering plant, in fruit, and when dead. This is the sort of awareness that you cannot get from a book; it can only be gained by experience. Moreover, don't worry about all those seemingly exciting plants that you heard about from the rain forest or from China: Learn about what you see every day. Even 20 miles away is too far. Get to know the plants in your own backyard, in your own neighborhood. Get to know them as friends. Ask questions regularly of whoever is teaching you. Begin to use one plant at a time in your meals—one plant that you absolutely, unequivocally know is an edible wild plant. You don't need to make entire meals from wild plants. Just begin by introducing one wild plant into your normal meals. You

might use the plant in a salad, in a soup, in a vegetable dish, or in a stew. Get to know it. Then, repeat this with another plant. Yes, at first you'll just be learning to recognize one plant at a time and getting to know it intimately, until you can spot it while driving by in a car.

- Believe it or not, most of what are called "common weeds" are edible and today are found worldwide. Thus, some of the likely plants you'll be tasting in the beginning will be plants such as lamb's quarter, sow thistle, purslane, curly dock, dandelion, chicory, cactus, acorns, watercress, cattails, onions, wild grasses, mustards, and so on.
- It is to your advantage to completely disregard any of the rules of thumb you've ever been taught about plant identification—you know, the shortcuts for determining whether or not a plant is edible: If a plant has a milky sap, it is not edible. If a plant causes an irritation in the mouth when you eat a little, it is not safe to eat. If the animals eat the plants or berries, they are safe to eat. If the berries are white, they are poisonous. If the berries are black or blue, they are safe to eat. And on and on. Disregard all these shortcuts because—although often based in some fact—they all have exceptions. There are no shortcuts to what is necessary: You must study, and you will need field experience.
- If there is any sort of shortcut to the study of plants, it is to learn to recognize plant families and learn to know which families are entirely safe for consumption. Beyond that, you must learn plants one by one for absolute safety.
- I strongly suggest that you take at least a college course in botany (preferably, taxonomy) so you get to know how botanists designate plant families. This will enable you to look at my list of safe families and then, by using the books written by botanists of the flora of your area, you can check to see which plants in your area belong to any of the completely safe families. After a while, this will come easy. Eventually, you'll look at a plant, examine it, and you'll know what family it likely belongs to.
- Again, there is no magical key that will make all of this effortless. Learn plants one by one, and then begin to learn the edible families one by one. Get a botanical flora book written for your area and study it. In California, that book is *The Jepson Manual: Vascular Plants of California* (2012).

Don't overlook the "weeds" in your own backyard, and seriously consider growing the "wild" foods and native plants in your own yard, rather than "ornamentals," which provide so little.

When you discover that we have ruined the planet Earth in the name of "modern agriculture" that produces inferior food, you will understand the meaning of Pogo's comment, "We have met the enemy, and he is us."

TEST YOUR KNOWLEDGE OF PLANTS

Here is a simple test that I use in my classes. Take the test for plants and mushrooms and see how you do.

1. ❒ True. ❒ False. Berries that glisten are poisonous.

2. ❒ True. ❒ False. White berries are all poisonous.

3. ❒ True. ❒ False. All blue and black berries are edible.

4. ❒ True. ❒ False. If uncertain about the edibility of berries, watch to see if the animals eat them. If the animals eat the berries, the berries are good for human consumption.

5. Would you follow this advice? State yes or no, and give a reason.

According to *Food in the Wilderness* authors George Martin and Robert Scott, "If you do not recognize a food as edible, chew a mouthful and keep it in the mouth. If it is very sharp, bitter, or distasteful, do not swallow it. If it tastes good, swallow only a little of the juice. Wait for about eight hours. If you have suffered no nausea, stomach or intestinal pains, repeat the same experiment swallowing a little more of the juice. Again, wait for eight hours. If there are no harmful results, it probably is safe for you to eat. (This test does not apply to mushrooms.)"

6. ❒ True. ❒ False. "A great number of wilderness plants are edible but generally they have very little food value." (Martin and Scott, ibid.)

7. ❒ True. ❒ False. Bitter plants are poisonous.

8. ❒ True. ❒ False. Plants that exude a milky sap when cut are all poisonous.

9. ❒ True. ❒ False. Plants that cause stinging or irritation on the skin are all unsafe for consumption.

10. The illustration to the right is the typical flower formation for all members of the Mustard family. Write out the formula:

    petal(s); sepal(s);

    stamen(s); pistil(s)

11. What is the value of being able to identify the Mustard family?

12. ❏ True. ❏ False. Mustard (used on hot dogs) is made by grinding up the yellow flowers of the mustard plant.

13. ❏ True. ❏ False. Yucca, century plant, and prickly pears are all members of the Cactus family.

14. ❏ True. ❏ False. There are no poisonous cacti.

15. ❏ True. ❏ False. Plants that resemble parsley, carrots, and fennel are all in the Parsley or Carrot family and thus are all safe to eat.

16. ❏ True. ❏ False. Only seventeen species of acorns are edible; the rest are toxic.

17. To consume acorns, the tannic acid must first be removed. Why?

18. If you are eating no meat or dairy products (during a survival situation, for example), how is it possible to get complete protein from plants alone?

19. ❏ True. ❏ False. There are no toxic grasses.

20. ❏ True. ❏ False. Seaweeds are unsafe survival foods.

21. ❏ True. ❏ False. All plants that have the appearance of a green onion and have the typical onion aroma can be safely eaten.

22. List all of the plant families (or groups) from this quiz that we've identified as entirely or primarily nontoxic:

ANSWERS

1. False. Insufficient data.

2. False. Though mostly true, there are exceptions, such as white strawberry, white mulberry, and others. Don't eat any berry unless you know its identity and you know it to be edible.

3. False. Mostly true, but there are some exceptions. Don't eat any berry unless you've identified it as an edible berry.

4. False, for several reasons. Certain animals are able to consume plants that would cause sickness or death in a human. Also, animals do occasionally die from eating poisonous plants—especially during times of drought. Also, just because you watched the animal eat a plant doesn't mean the animal didn't get sick later!

5. Very bad advice, even though this has been repeated endlessly in "survival manuals" and magazine articles. Because food is rarely your top "survival priority," this is potentially dangerous advice.

6. False. To verify that this is untrue, look at *Composition of Foods*, which is published by the US Department of Agriculture. In many cases, wild foods are far more nutritious than common domesticated foods.

7. False. Insufficient data. Many bitter plants are rendered edible and palatable simply by cooking or boiling.

8. False. Though you can't eat any of the euphorbias, many others (like dandelion, lettuce, milkweed, sow thistle, etc.) exude a milky sap. Forget about such "shortcuts." Get to know the individual plants.

9. False. Many edible plants have stickers or thorns that must first be removed, or cooked away, such as nettles and cacti.

10. Mustard flowers are composed of 4 sepals (one under each petal); 4 petals (the colorful part of the flower); 1 pistil (in the very center of flower, the female part of the flower); and 6 stamens (which surround the pistil), 4 are tall, and 2 are short.

11. There are no poisonous members of the Mustard family.

12. False. The mustard condiment is made by grinding the seeds. Yellow is typically from food coloring.

13. False. Only the prickly pear is a cactus.

14. True, but you must know what is, and is not, a cactus. There are some very bitter narcotic cacti that you would not eat due to unpalatability. Also, some euphorbias closely resemble cacti and will cause sickness if eaten. Euphorbias

exude a milky sap when cut; cacti do not. Any fleshy, palatable part of true cacti can be eaten.

15. False. The Carrot family contains both good foods and deadly poisons. Never eat any wild plant resembling parsley unless you have identified that specific plant as an edible species.

16. False. All acorns can be consumed once the tannic acid is removed.

17. Tannic acid is bitter.

18. Combine the seeds from grasses with the seeds from legumes. This generally produces a complete protein. For more details, see *Diet for a Small Planet* by Frances Moore Lappé.

Traditional Diets That Combine Legumes and Grass Seeds to Make a Complete Protein

Loosely based upon "Summary of Complementary Protein Relationships," Chart X in *Diet for a Small Planet* by Frances Moore Lappé

	Legumes	Grasses
Asian diet	Soy (miso, tofu, etc.)	Rice
Mexican diet	Beans (black beans, etc.)	Corn (tortillas)
Middle East diet	Garbanzos	Wheat
Southern United States	Black-eyed peas	Grits
Starving student	Peanut butter	Wheat bread
Others to consider	Mesquite, palo verde, peas, carob, etc.	Millet, rye, oats, various wild grasses, etc.

19. True; however, be certain that the seeds are mature and have no mold-like growth on them.

20. False. Seaweeds are excellent. Make certain they've not been rotting on the beach, and don't collect near any sewage treatment facilities.

21. True. However, be sure you have an onion!

22. All members of the Mustard family, all palatable cacti, all acorns, all cattails, grasses, seaweeds, onions. There are many other "safe" families, but you will need to do a bit of botanical study to identify those families. Begin by reading the descriptions of each family in this book. Also, consider reading *Botany in a Day: The Patterns Method of Plant Identification* by Tom Elpel.

THE DOZEN EASIEST-TO-RECOGNIZE, MOST-WIDESPREAD, MOST-VERSATILE WILD FOODS OF CALIFORNIA

In the mid-1970s, I began to investigate the edibility of whole plant families and found that there were quite a few entire families that are safe to eat, given a few considerations in each case. Some of these families are difficult to recognize unless you are a trained botanist. Still, in this book I have described many of the entirely safe families. My original research on this was done with Dr. Leonid Enari, who was one of my teachers and the chief botanist at the Los Angeles County Arboretum in Arcadia, California.

The chart below was the idea of my friend Jay Watkins, who long urged me to produce a simple handout on the dozen most-common edible plants that every-one should know. Granted, there are many more than a dozen, but as Jay and I discussed this idea, I decided to focus on twelve plants that could be found not just any-where in the United States but in most locales throughout the world. The result is largely self-explanatory. This chart assumes that you already know these plants, because its purpose is not identification. Anyone who has studied wild foods for a few years is probably already familiar with all these plants. However, not everyone is aware that these plants are found worldwide.

This overview should help both beginners and specialists. It is a simple comparative chart that could be expanded to many, many pages, but I've deliberately kept it short and simple.

Cattail

	Description	Parts used	Food uses	Preparation	Benefits	Where found	When found
Acorns	Fruit of the oak tree	Acorns (nuts)	Flour, pickles, mush	Leach out tannic acid first, then grind	Similar to potatoes	Mountains, valleys	Fall
Cacti	Succulent desert plants of various shapes	1. Tender parts; 2. fruit	1. Salad; cooked vegetable; omelet; 2. Dessert; drinks	1. Carefully remove spines; 2. Dice or slice as needed	Pads said to be good for diabetics; fruits rich in sugar	Dry, desertlike environments; Mediterranean zones	Young green pads in spring and summer; fruit in summer and fall
Cattail	Reedlike plants; fruit looks like hot dog on a stick	1. Pollen; 2. Green flower spike; 3. Tender shoots; 4. Rhizome	1. Flour; 2. Cooked vegetable; 3. Salad; 4. Flour	1. Shake out pollen; 2. Boil; 3. Remove outer green fibrous parts; 4. Remove outer parts and crush	Widespread, versatile	Wet areas (e.g., roadside ditches, marshes)	Spring through fall
Chickweed	Weak-stemmed, opposite leaves, 5-petaled flower	Entire tender plant	Salad or tea	Rinse and add dressing; or make infusion	Good diuretic	Common and widespread when moisture is present	Spring and summer
Curly Dock	Long leaves with wavy margins	1. Leaves; 2. Stems; 3. Seeds	1. Salad; cooked vegetable; 2. Pie; 3. Flour	1. Clean; 2. Use like rhubarb; 3. Winnow seeds	Richer in vitamin C than oranges	Common in fields and near water	Spring through fall
Dandelion	Low plant, toothed leaves, conspicuous yellow flower	1. Roots; 2. Leaves	1. Cooked vegetable; coffee-like beverage; 2. Salad or cooked vegetable	1. Clean and cook; or dry, roast, grind; 2. Clean and make desired dish	Richest source of beta carotene; very high in vitamin A	Common in lawns and fields	Best harvested in spring

Plant	Description	Parts Used	Uses	Preparation	Benefits	Habitat	Season
Grasses	Many widespread varieties	1. Seeds; 2. Leaves	1. Flour and mush; 2. Salad; juiced; cooked vegetable	1. Harvest and winnow; 2. Harvest, clean, and chop	1. Easy to store; 2. Rich in many nutrients	Common in all environments	1. Fall; 2. Spring
Lamb's Quarter	Triangular leaves with toothed margins, mealy surface	1. Leaves and tender stems; 2. Seeds	1. Salad; soup; omelets; 2. Bread; mush	1. Harvest; clean; 2. Winnow	Rich in vitamin A and calcium	Likes disturbed, rich soils	Spring through fall
Mustard	Variable leaves with large terminal lobes; 4-petaled flowers	Leaves, seeds, some roots	Salads; cooked dishes; seasoning	Gather, clean, and cut as needed	Said to help prevent cancer	Common in fields and many environments	Spring through fall
Onions	Grasslike appearance; flowers with 3 petals and 3 sepals	Leaves, bulbs	Seasoning; salad; soup; vegetable dishes	Clean, remove tough outer leaves	Good for reducing high blood pressure and high cholesterol levels	Some varieties found in all environments	Spring is best
Purslane	Low-growing succulent, paddle-shaped leaves	All tender portions	Salad; sautéed; pickled; soup; vegetable dishes	Rinse off any soil	Richest known plant source of omega-3 fatty acids	Common in parks, gardens, disturbed soils	Summer
Seaweeds	Marine algae of many shapes and colors	Entire plant	Depends on seaweed: salad, soup, stew, broth	Use dried, raw, or cooked, depending on species	Excellent source of iodine; great salt substitute	Oceans	Year-round

Latin Names: Acorns = *Quercus* spp.; Cacti = Cactacea (Cactus family); Cattail = *Typha* spp.; Chickweed = *Stellaria media*; Curly Dock = *Rumex crispus*; Dandelion = *Taraxacum officinale*; Grasses = Poaceae (Grass family); Lamb's quarter = *Chenopodium album*; Mustard (Mustard family Brassicaceae) = *Brassica* spp.; Onions = *Allium* spp.; Purslane = *Portulaca oleracea*; Seaweeds = brown, red, and marine green algae (Phaeophyta, Rhodophyta, Chlorophyta).

STAFF OF LIFE:
BEST WILD-FOOD BREAD SOURCES

The baking of bread goes back to the most ancient cultures on the Earth, back when humankind discovered that you could grind up the seeds of grasses, add a few other ingredients, let it rise, and bake it. There are countless variations, of course, but bread was once so nutritious that it was called the "staff of life."

Most likely the discovery of bread predated agriculture, because the Earth was full of wild grasses and a broad assortment of roots and seeds that could be baked into nutritious loaves. Most grains store well for a long time, which allowed people the time to pursue culture, inner growth, and technology. The development of civilizations and the development of agriculture go hand in hand, and bread was right there from the beginning.

Today, we are at another extreme of a very long road of human development. We started with the struggle for survival, with the surplus of the land allowing us

RECIPES

Beginner Wild Bread

1 cup whole wheat flour

1 cup wild flour of your choice

3 teaspoons baking powder

3 tablespoons honey

1 egg

1 cup milk

3 tablespoons oil

Salt to taste, if desired

Mix all ingredients well and bake in oiled pans for about 45 minutes at 250°F or in your solar oven until done.

Beginner Pancake Recipe

Follow the above recipe, adding extra milk or water until you have a pancake batter consistency. Make pancakes as normal.

the time to develop more fully in all aspects. That good bread from the Earth was heavy, rich, extremely nutritious. It was a vitamin and mineral tablet.

We produced so much grain that the United States called itself "the breadbasket of the world." And this massive volume resulted in losses from insects in the fields and also due to spoilage. Then came the so-called "Green Revolution" where chemical fertilizers replaced time-honored ones such as animal manures, straw and hay, compost, bonemeal, and other such natural substances that the modern farmer was too busy and too modern to use. Crops increased while the nutritional values dropped. Though this is a gross oversimplification, bread from the supermarket is no longer the staff of life. The mineral content of the once-rich soils of the United States has steadily declined. Producers process and refine "white flour" and then add certain minerals back in to the flour itself. We sacrificed quality, as we thought it would bring us security, and we knew it would bring big bucks. Now the great irony is that we have lost the quality of the food, of the soil, and, ultimately, we are no more secure than we ever were. Why? Because a soil rich in natural organic matter can withstand floods and droughts and the ravages of insects. It is the folly of man that causes the droughts and plagues of modern times.

There is much—very much—that we need to learn about modern agriculture, or "agribiz," as it is more appropriately called. We should not put our heads into the sand, ostrich-like, and pretend the problem does not exist.

Curly dock

Personal solutions are many. Grow your own garden. Learn about wild foods and use them daily.

By using common wild plants, you can actually create nutritious breads that are comparable to the breads your ancestors ate. The easiest way to get started is to make flour from these wild seeds and mix that flour 50-50 with your conventional flours, such as wheat. You'll end up with a more-flavorful, more-nutritious bread, pancake, or pastry product. Moreover, once you begin to use your local wild grains, you'll be amazed at how tasty, how abundant, and how versatile these wild foods are.

The chart on page 247, is by no means complete. It is a general guideline to show you what is available over widespread areas. However, there are quite a few plants of limited range that produce abundant seeds or other parts suitable for bread making.

Note that "Grass" is a huge category, as it actually includes many of our domestic grains such as wheat, corn, rye, and barley. Though some of the seeds listed in this chart can be eaten raw, most require some processing before you can eat them. Acorns must be soaked or boiled to get rid of all the bitter tannic acid. Agave and yucca seeds and fruits are bitter and soapy and must be cooked first. The seed from amaranth, dock, and lamb's quarter can get somewhat bitter and astringent as it gets older; it is improved by cooking.

By rediscovering the wealth of wild plants that are found throughout this country, we can bring bread back to its status as the "staff of life."

"Wild Bread" Chart

	Parts used	How processed	Where found	Palatability	Ability to store
Acorns	Shelled acorns	Leach acorns of tannic acid by soaking or boiling and grind into meal	Worldwide; ripens in fall	Good, if fully leached	Excellent
Agave	Seeds and fruits	Seeds boiled and ground; fruits boiled and mashed	Southwest US, Mexico, and dry environments	Good if cooked	Very good
Amaranth	Seeds	Collect and winnow seeds	Worldwide as a weed of disturbed soils	Very good	Very good
Cactus	Seeds	Mash ripe fruits, pour through colander to extract seeds	Throughout US, though most common in Mediterranean climates worldwide	Good	Good
Cattail	Pollen and rhizome	Shake the top of cattail spikes into bag to collect pollen; mash peeled rhizome and separate out fiber	Worldwide in wet and marshy areas	Very good	Good
Dock	Seeds	Collect brown seeds in fall, rub to remove "wings"; winnow	Worldwide in wet areas and disturbed soils	Acceptable	Very good
Grass (most species)	Seeds	Generally, simply collect and winnow; difficulty depends on species	Worldwide, some found in nearly every environment	Generally very good	Very good to excellent
Lamb's Quarter	Seeds	Collect when leaves on plant are dry; rub between hands, winnow	Worldwide in disturbed soils and farm soils	Acceptable to good	Very good
Mesquite	Entire pod	The entire pod is ground into flour	Widespread throughout Southwest	Excellent	Very good
Wild Buckwheat	Entire seed heads	Collect entire mature head, pick out stems, grind	Western US and Mediterranean climates	Very good	Very good
Yucca	Seeds and fruit	Collect black seed from mature fruit and grind; mash up fruit when insides are still white	Southwestern US and northern Mexico	Acceptable	Very good

Note: This chart is intended only as a general guideline to compare sources for "wild bread" ingredients. There may be many other wild plants that can be used for bread. Never eat any wild plant that you have not positively identified as an edible species.

Latin names: Acorns = *Quercus* spp.; Agave = *Agave* spp.; Amaranth = *Amaranthus* spp.; Cactus = primarily *Opuntia* spp. and other Cactaceae; Cattail = *Typha* spp.; Curly Dock = *Rumex crispus*; Grass = Poaceae (family); Lamb's quarter = *Chenopodium album*; Mesquite = *Prosopis glandulosa*; California buckwheat = *Eriogonum fasciculatum*; Yucca = *Hesperoyucca* spp.

SWEET TOOTH:
BEST WILD-FOOD SUGARS AND DESSERTS

When people speak of sugar today, they are almost always speaking of the highly refined, nutrition-less white substance made from sugarcane or sugar beets. Unfortunately, modern sugar is a foodless food. It is the cocaine of the modern human's dinner plate. It is not good for the body, and it offers no nutrients whatsoever. It has not always been so.

Just a few generations ago, it was common for people to make their own sugars. Every culture had its favorite sources for their sugars, depending on what was found in the wild or what was grown in that particular location. In most cases, they simply collected, dried, and ground up sugar-rich fruits. Most such fruits will naturally crystallize with time and then could be further ground. The advantage of these sugars over white cane sugar is that these sugars had their own individual flavors, and they contained many valuable minerals.

Some sugars are quite simple to produce, such as honey. Its main obstacles are to find a way to house the bees—something modern beekeepers do quite well—and to keep from getting stung. And tapping maple trees (and several other trees) was so simple that even the North American natives did it. They simply cut narrow slashes into the tree, inserted hollow tubes made from elder branches, and collected the sap in whatever containers they had. Raw maple sap is usually boiled down to get a syrup of the desired consistency and sugar content. Sometimes you boil off about 40 gallons of water for each gallon of syrup. You do *not* do this indoors.

People have always sought ways to make foods more flavorful, and sugar is certainly useful in that regard. However, sugar is also valuable as a preservative. Both sugar and salt help to preserve foods and keep them from spoiling. This was especially important in the past when there was no electricity or refrigerators.

It's amazing how fast a modern culture forgets things. Probably not one in a thousand urbanites knows these simple details about sugar. Our culture has sunk to such ignorance in this matter that we somehow believe that the only choice is between white sugar, the pink container, or the blue packet. Rather than produce nutritious sugars as we had in the past, the trend is to produce high-tech sweet substances that not only have no nutrients but have no calories either, as does white sugar. The wonders of science never cease!

For those of you who want to try making sugar, the following chart gives you some ideas as to what is available. Currants and gooseberries were very popular among Native Americans, not as a sweetener but as a preservative. They ground their jerky and added crushed currants or gooseberries, and the result was pemmican.

Though many of the wild berries described in the chart have been used as sweeteners for other foods, most of them are good in their own right and have long been used to make such things as drinks, pies, jams, custard, and a variety of dessert items. Details for these can be found in many of the wild-food cookbooks available.

Here's one recipe that can be used with all of the sugars on the chart except carob, maple, and manzanita; these three are not fleshy berries, so they won't cook up like the others.

RECIPE

Appalachian Brickle

½ gallon ripe toyon berries

Water to cover berries

½ cup honey

Approximately ⅓ cup biscuit mix

Begin by gently cooking the washed berries in just enough water to cover them. When they are cooked, pour off the water, add fresh water, and cook a little longer. Then add just a little water, add the honey, and stir. After the mixture thickens, add the biscuit mix, little by little, and stir. The mix will be very thick when it is ready to serve.

This makes a heavy, sweet dessert. In the old days, what wasn't eaten of this would be put into a bread pan and baked until dry so it would store. It would then last a long time until reconstituted. The dried shape looked like a brick, which is the source of the name.

Sweet Tooth: Best Wild-Food Sugars and Desserts

	Part used	How processed	Where found	Sweetness/palatability	Ability to store
Apples, Wild (including crab apples)	Whole fruit	Use fresh, or slice, dry, and grind to flour	Entire US	Very good; collect when ripe	Very good
Berries (black-, rasp-, thimbleberries)	Whole fruit	Use fresh, or dry and grind	Entire US	Excellent	Very good
Carob	Whole pod	Remove seeds, grind entire pod; use fresh or dried	Southern half of US, Mediterranean climates	Good; rich source of calcium	Very good
Currants	Whole fruit	Use fresh, or dry and store	Entire US	Good	Very good
Elderberry	Whole fruit	Use fresh if cooked first; or dry and store	Entire US	Contains sugar but tart	Good
Gooseberries	Whole fruit	Remove spiny layer, then use fresh or dried	Entire US	Good	Very good
Grape, Wild	Whole fruit	Use fresh or dried	Most of the US	Sometimes tart; collect ripe fruit	Very good
Manzanita	Whole fruit	Dry and grind the pulp around the seed, but not the seed	Southwestern US	A bit tart; used like aspic	Good
Maple	Sap	Cut bark on tree, capture sap; use fresh; crystallizes naturally	Entire US, but flows best where there is snow	Excellent	Excellent
Prickly Pear Cactus	Fruit	Remove stickers, use inner pulp fresh or dried, with or without seed	Entire US, but most common in Southwest	Excellent	Good
Toyon	Fruit	Cook and use fresh, or dry for storage	Southwest	Good, a bit tart	Very good

Note: There are many sugars found in nature, usually in the fruits. Honey is a traditional sugar, made indirectly from plant nectars. Other traditional sugars include dried and powdered dates, dried pomegranate juice, and beets. This chart compares a few wild sugar sources that are the most widespread throughout North America. There are many plants that are either marginal sugar sources or available in very limited locations. Never use any wild plant for sugar or food until you have positively identified it as an edible plant.

Latin names: Apples = *Malus* spp.; Berries = *Rubus* spp.; Carob = *Ceratonia siliqua*; Elderberry = *Sambucus* spp.; Currants and Gooseberries = *Ribes* spp.; Grape, wild = *Vitis* spp.; Manzanita = *Arctostaphylos* spp.; Maple = *Acer* spp.; Prickly pear cactus = *Opuntia* spp.; Toyon = *Heteromeles arbutifolia*.

USEFUL REFERENCES

Anderson, M. Kat. *Tending the Wild: Native American Knowledge and the Management of California's Natural Resources.* Berkeley: University of California Press, 2005. A fantastic reference on how Native Americans used fire and other means for passive agriculture.

Angier, Bradford. *Free for the Eating.* Mechanicsburg, PA: Stackpole Books, 1996.

Arora, David. *All That the Rain Promises and More: A Hip Pocket Guide to Western Mushrooms.* Berkeley, CA: 10 Speed Press, 1991. This is a condensed mushroom ID book for those living in California and the western states.

————. *Mushrooms Demystified.* Berkeley, CA: 10 Speed Press, 1986. There are many books out there about mycology—this is the one I use. This is 958 pages of comprehensive explanations, keys, and photos.

Baldwin, Bruce G., et al., eds. *The Jepson Manual: Vascular Plants of California,* second edition. Berkeley: University of California Press, 2012.

Bean, Lowell John, and Katherine Siva Saubel. *Temalpakh: Cahuilla Indian Knowledge and Usage of Plants.* Banning, CA: Malki Museum Press, 1972. A wonderful original sourcebook on how the Native Americans around Palm Springs traditionally used plants. A great section on mesquite and acorns.

Brenzel, Kathleen Norris, ed. *Sunset Western Garden Book.* New York: Time Home Entertainment, 2013. By the editors of Sunset Books and *Sunset* magazine, yes, this is about plants in your garden, but there's a lot of relevant, useful information in this book!

Campbell, Paul Douglas. *Survival Skills of Native California.* Salt Lake City, UT: Gibbs Smith, 1999. This book includes a treasure trove of information about how people in California actually did things, along with a large section on plant uses.

Clarke, Oscar. *Flora of the Santa Ana River and Environs.* Berkeley, CA: Heyday Books, 2007.

Cornett, James. *How Indians Used Desert Plants*. Palm Springs, CA: Nature Trails Press, 2002. A slim book with good photos and good treatments of the common desert plants.

Doyle, Harrison. *Golden Chia: Ancient Indian Energy Food*. Vista, CA: Hillside Press, 1973.

Dunmire, William, and Gail Tierney. *Wild Plants of the Pueblo Province: Exploring Ancient and Enduring Uses*. Santa Fe: Museum of New Mexico Press, 1995. A good historical account of how plants were used in the pueblos, mostly in New Mexico.

Elpel, Tom. *Botany in a Day: The Patterns Method of Plant Identification*. Pony, MT: HOPS Press, 2000.

———. *Participating in Nature: Wilderness Survival and Primitive Living Skills*. Pony, MT: HOPS Press, 2009.

Garcia, Cecelia, and Dr. James Adams. *Healing with Medicinal Plants of the West: Cultural and Scientific Basis for Their Use*. La Crescenta, CA: Abedus Press, 2005. An excellent summary of the common edible and medicinal plant uses found in California.

Gibbons, Euell. *Stalking the Blue-Eyed Scallop*. New York: David McKay, 1964. A good description of many of the foods found on the Pacific Coast.

Kane, Charles. *Herbal Medicine of the American Southwest: A Guide to the Medicinal and Edible Plants of the Southwestern United States*. Tucson, AZ: Lincoln Town Press, 2006. Good descriptions and photos of plants found widely throughout the Southwest.

Kirk, Donald. *Wild Edible Plants of Western North America*. Happy Camp, CA: Naturegraph, 1970. Though you generally cannot positively identify plants with this book, it does contain more edible and useful plants than any other single book on the subject that I'm aware of.

Knute, Adrienne. *Plants of the East Mojave*, second edition, Barstow, CA: Mojave River Valley Museum Association, 2002. Good photos of the desert plants.

Moerman, Daniel E. *Native American Ethnobotany.* Portland, OR: Timber Press, 1998. Nearly a thousand pages of descriptions of how every plant known to be used by Native Americans was utilized. No pictures at all, but lots of useful data.

Nyerges, Christopher. *Foraging Wild Edible Plants of North America.* Guilford, CT: FalconGuides, 2016. An all-color guide to plants that are widespread in North America, with lots of recipes.

———. *Nuts and Berries of California.* Guilford, CT: FalconGuides, 2015. An excellent companion book to *Foraging California.*

Watt, Bernice, and Annabel Merrill. *Agriculture Handbook No. 8, Composition of Foods: Raw, Processed, Prepared.* USDA, 1963.

INDEX

A
Acacia, 120
Acacia dealbata, 121-122
Acacia spp., 120
Adoxaceae, 48
Agavaceae, 207
Aizoaceae, 52
Alliaceae, 211
Allium spp., 211
Althaea officinalis, 151
Amaranth, 55
Amaranthaceae, 55
Amaranth family, 55
Amaranthus spp., 55
Apiaceae, 58
Arctostaphylos spp., 117
Arecaceae, 215
Arrow shafts, 139, 186
Ascomycetes, 27
Asteraceae, 61
Atriplex californica, 103

B
Basidiomycetes, 18
Bay, California, 44
Bitter cherry, 184
Blackberry, 189
Black nightshade, 193
Black walnut, 141
Bracken, 34
Bracken family, 34
Brassica spp., 73
Brassicaceae, 73
Bread sources, wild, 247
Brickle, Appalachian, 249
Brill, Steven, 35
Brown algae, 30

Buckthorn family, 179
Buckwheat, California, 165
Buckwheat family, 165
Bush mallow, 150

C
Cactaceae, 93
Cactus family, 93
Cakile edentula, 76
Cakile maritima, 76
Calanthus inflatus, 79
California bay, 44
California buckwheat, 165
California coffee berry, 179
California fan palm, 216
Capsella bursa-pastoris, 82
Carob, 107
Carrot family, 58
Caryophyllaceae, 99
Catalina Island cherry, 184
Cattail, 228
Cattail family, 228
Century plant family, 207
Ceratonia siliqua, 123
Checker mallow, 150
Cheeseweed, 150
Chenopodiaceae, 103
Chenopodium album, 106
Chenopodium californicum, 108
Chenopodium murale, 106
Cherries, wild, 183
Chia, 146
Chicken-of-the-Woods, 18
Chickweed, 99
Chicory, 61
Chlorophyllum rhacodes, 23
Chokecherry, western, 184

Cichorium intybus, 61
Claytonia perfoliata, 152
Cochineal beetle, 93
Coffee berry, California, 179
Coffee substitute, 63, 66, 68, 69, 72
Commelina benghalensis, 221
Commelinaceae, 219
Coprinus comatus, 21
Crassulaceae, 115
Curly dock, 168
Currants, 138

D
Dandelion, 70
Dennstaedtiacea, 34
Desert candle (aka Indian cabbage), 79
Desert portulaca, 176
Diabetes, 96
Diarrhea, 185, 190
Dock, curly, 168
Dolma, 151, 198
Dudleya spp., 115

E
Easy-to-recognize wild foods, 241
Elderberry, 48
Ephedraceae, 38
Ephedra family, 38
Ephedra spp., 38
Ericaceae, 117
Eriogonum fasciculatum, 165
Erodium spp., 136
EUDICOTS, 47
Euphorbia, 93
Euphorbia peplus, 99

F
Fabaceae, 120
Fagaceae, 132
Fan palm, California, 216

Fennel, 58
FERNS, 33
Fiber source, 130, 135, 202, 207, 226
Fiddlehead, 35
Fig marigold family, 52
Filaree, 136
Foeniculum vulgare, 58
Frangula californica, 179
Frangula purshiana, 179

G
Garlic family, 211
Geraniaceae, 136
Geranium family, 136
Gibbons, Euell, 1, 229
Glasswort, 109
Gooseberries, 138
Gooseberry family, 138
Goosefoot family, 103
Gramineae, 225
Grape family, 203
Grape, wild, 203
Grass family, 225
Green algae, 30
Grifolia sulphureus, 18
Grossulariaceae, 138
GYMNOSPERMS, 37

H
Headaches, 46, 50
Heath family, 117
Hedge mustard, 90
Hesperoyucca whipplei, 207
Heteromeles arbutifolia, 181
Holly leaf cherry, 184

I
Indian cabbage, 79
Inky Cap, 21
Insulation, 231

J

Jojoba, 191
Jojoba family, 191
Juglandaceae, 141
Juglans californica, 141
Juglans hindsii, 141
Juncaceae, 223
Juncus textilis, 223

L

Lactuca serriola et al., 64
Laetiporus sulphureus, 18
Lamb's quarter, 106
Lamiaceae, 144
Lappé, Frances Moore, 240
Lauraceae, 44
Laurel family, 44
Laxative, 179, 180
Legume family, 120
Lepiota, 23
Lepiota rhacodes, 23
Live-forever, 115
London rocket, 90
Lopseed family, 161

M

Macrolepiota rhacodes, 23
MAGNOLIIDS, 43
Malacothamnus sp., 150
Mallow, 149
Mallow family, 149
Malvaceae, 149
Malva neglecta, 149
Manzanita, 117
Marshmallow, 151
Mentha spp., 144
Mesquite, 129
Mimulus, common, 161
Mimulus guttatus, 161
Miner's lettuce, 152
Miner's lettuce family, 152
Mint, 144

Mint family, 144
Monkey flower, 161
MONOCOTS, 206
Montiaceae, 152
Morchella esculenta, 27
Morels, 27
Mormon tea, 38
Mulga, 121
MUSHROOMS, 15
Muskroot family, 48
Mustard, 73
Mustard family, 73
Mustard flower formula, 164
Mustard, hedge, 90
Mycology, 16, 232

N

Nasturtium, 196
Nasturtium family, 196
Nasturtium officinale, 84
Nettle family, 199
Nettle, stinging, 199
New Zealand spinach, 52
Nightshade, black, 193
Nightshade family, 193
Nightshade, western, 193
Nopales, 94, 96
Nutritional data, 12

O

Oak tree, 132
Oak family, 132
Oca, 156
Omega-3 fatty acids, 178
Onion family, 211
Onions, wild, 211
Opuntia spp., 93
Orach, 103
Oxalidaceae, 155
Oxalis family, 155
Oxalis spp., 155
Oyster Mushroom, 25

P

Palm, California fan, 216
Palm family, 215
Palo verde, 126
Parkinsonia microphylla, 126
Parkinsonia florida, 126
Parthenocissus, 203
Passiflora caerulea, 158
Passiflora tarminiana, 158
Passifloraceae, 158
Passionflower, 158
Passionflower family, 158
Phrymaceae, 161
Pickleweed, 109
Pinaceae, 41
Pine, 41
Pine family, 41
Pink family, 99
Pinus spp., 41
Plantaginaceae, 163
Plantain family, 163
Pleurotus ostreatus, 25
Poaceae, 225
Poison oak remedy, 119
Polygonaceae, 165
Polyporus sulfureus, 18
Portulacaceae, 176
Portulaca, desert, 176
Portulaca halimoides, 176
Portulaca oleracea, 176
Prickly lettuce, 64
Prickly pear, 93
Prosopis glandulosa, 129
Prosopis pubescens, 129
Prunus spp., 183
Pteridium aquilinum, 34
Purslane, 176
Purslane family, 176

Q

Quercus ilex, 152
Quercus spp., 152

R

Radish, wild, 87
Raphanus raphanistrum, 87
Raphanus sativus, 87
Raspberry, 189
Red algae, 30
Rhamnaceae, 179
Rhubarb, wild, 174
Ribes spp., 138
Rosaceae, 181
Rosa spp., 186
Rose family, 181
Rose, wild, 186
Rubus spp., 189
Rumex acetosella, 172
Rumex crispus, 168
Rumex hymenosepalus, 174
Rush, 223
Rush family, 223
Russian thistle, 112

S

Salicornia spp., 109
Salsola tragus, 112
Salsola kali, 112
Salvia columbariae, 146
Sambucus spp., 48
Scarlet pimpernel, 99
Screwbean, 129
Sea rocket, 76
SEAWEEDS, 29
Sedative, 160
Shaggy Mane, 21
Sheep sorrel, 172
Shepherd's purse, 82
Sidalcea sp., 150
Simmondsiaceae, 191
Simmondsia chinensis, 191
Sisymbrium irio, 90
Sisymbrium officinale, 90
Soap plants, 108, 207, 208
Soaproot, 108

Solanaceae, 193
Solanum americanum, 193
Solanum douglasii, 193
Solanum nigrum, 193
Solanum nodiflorum, 193
Solanum xanti, 193
Sonchus oleraceus et al., 67
Sorrel, sheep, 172
Sorrel, wood, 155
Sour grass, 155
Sow thistle, 67
Speedwell, 163
Spiderwort family, 219
Spiderwort, tropical, 221
Spurge, 99, 100, 176
Stellaria media, 99
Stinging nettle, 199
Stonecrop family, 115
Sugar sources, wild, 248
Sunflower family, 61

T

Taraxacum officinale, 70
Test your knowledge of plants, 237
Tetragonia tetragonioides, 52
Thimbleberry, 189
Tinder, 231
Tobacco alternative, 119
Toyon, 181
Tradescantia fluminensis, 219
Tropaeolaceae, 196
Tropaeolum majus, 196
Tropical spiderwort, 221
Tumbleweed, 113
Typhaceae, 228
Typha spp., 228

U

Umbellularia californica, 44
Urticaceae, 199
Urtica dioica, 199

V

Veronica, 163
Veronica americana, 163
Vinegar substitute, 119
Vitaceae, 203
Vitis spp., 203

W

Walnut, black, 141
Walnut family, 141
Wandering Jew, 219
Washingtonia filifera, 216
Watercress, 84
Western chokecherry, 184
Western nightshade, 193
Wild radish, 87
Wild cherries, 183
Wild grape, 203
Wild onions, 211
Wild rhubarb, 174
Wild rose, 186
Wood sorrel, 155

Y

Yellow Monkey Flower, 161
Yucca, 207
Yucca spp., 208

RECIPE INDEX

Acorns
Tongva Memories, 134

Chickweed
Mia's Chickweed Soup, 101

Curly Dock
Curly Dock "Nori" (Vegetable Chips), 171

Elderberry/flower
Elderberry Sauce, 51
Elder Flower Vinegar, 49

Filaree
Filaree Juice, 137

Flour
Beginner Pancake Recipe, 244
Beginner Wild Bread, 244

Hedge mustard
Screaming at the Moon, 91
Tumbled Rice, 114

Lemons
Lemon and Wild Passion Fruit Marmalade, 159

Mesquite
Traditional Southern California Mesquite Bean Cake, 130

Miner's lettuce
Richard's Salad, 154

Mustard
Pascal's Mustard, 75

Nasturtium
Nasturtium "Brain Food" Capers, 198

New Zealand spinach
Moon Sets in the Malibu Lagoon, The, 54

Onion
Saturday Night Special, 86

Purslane
Purslane Salsa, 178

Radish
Pickled Radish Pods, 89

Russian thistle
Tumbled Rice, 114

Sea rocket
"Wasabi," 77

Sheep sorrel
Shiyo's Garden Salad, 173

Sow thistle
Spring Awakening, 69

Stinging nettles
Stinging Nettles Hot Sauce, 200

Toyon
Appalachian Brickle, 249
Chumash Winter, 182

Watercress
Saturday Night Special, 86

Wild Passion Fruit
Lemon and Wild Passion Fruit Marmalade, 159

Yucca
Pickled Yucca Shoots, 209

ABOUT THE AUTHOR

Christopher Nyerges, cofounder of the School of Self-Reliance, has led wild-food walks for thousands of students since 1974. He has authored more than a dozen books on wild foods, survival, and self-reliance, as well as thousands of newspaper and magazine articles. He continues to teach where he lives in Los Angeles County, California. More information about his classes and seminars is available atSchoolofSelf-Reliance.com, on Facebook, or by writing to School of Self-Reliance, Box 41834, Eagle Rock, CA 90041.

Other Books by Christopher Nyerges
Nuts and Berries of California (a companion to Foraging California)
Foraging Oregon
Foraging Washington
Foraging Idaho
Foraging Edible Wild Plants of North America
Guide to Wild Foods and Useful Plants
Testing Your Outdoor Survival Skills
How to Survive Anywhere
Self-Sufficient Home
Extreme Simplicity
Enter the Forest